D0308475

Praise for
How to be an Amazing Middle Leader

How to be an Amazing Middle Leader is a very inspiring read, with relevant anecdotes and useful tips with puzzling questions to reflect upon. The 5 As questionnaire identified my characteristics and helped me review on how I respond to day-to-day situations. I now have great ideas on how to use 'pupil talk' more effectively in my department and across the school.

Reahgan Quartermaine,
PE advanced skills teacher and GCSE coordinator

How can middle leaders be an outstanding practitioner, proactive manager and visionary leader? With her calm, authoritative narrative, Caroline Bentley-Davies mentors you through the myriad of skills, such as the art of delegation as well as balancing the needs of your team versus the pressures of school improvement, that are indispensable for a busy middle leader today. As an experienced head of department, I feel refreshed and rejuvenated after reading it: Caroline Bentley-Davies provides an excellent mix of advice when undertaking this daunting, demanding, exhilarating role and opportunities for reflection on your journey towards being an outstanding middle leader – this is professional learning at its best.

Dawn German, head of modern languages,
The Clere School, Hampshire

I really enjoyed the easy-to-access structure; you can dip in and out of it as well as read it from cover to cover. Very handy chapter titles, reflection points and relevant content. I particularly liked the quiz at the beginning which really made me focus on myself and my development instead of just learning about someone else's experience. Very refreshing. Very current and salient points regarding leadership and management too. Caroline's experiences are so relevant. Also enjoyed the 'What not to do' section which provided an amusing but sensible reminder not to fall into any traps – we all know a few of the huge characters Caroline mentions!

Kate Lewis, head of English,
Arthur Mellows Village College, Peterborough

This amazing book is a must read for anyone who aspires to be a high-performing middle leader. A concise, practical read that provides middle leaders with the strategies to ensure they have day-to-day impact in this crucial and challenging role. Bentley-Davies covers the role from every angle, from how to drive consistent teacher quality, through to how to effect long term change and influence whole school behaviours, this book delivers on it all. An essential read for any outstanding middle leader.

Sarah Martin, associate principal and
teaching and learning leader, Academies Enterprise Trust

How to be an

Amazing Middle Leader

How to be an

Amazing Middle Leader

Caroline Bentley-Davies

Crown House Publishing Limited
www.crownhouse.co.uk
www.crownhousepublishing.com

First published by

Crown House Publishing Ltd
Crown Buildings, Bancyfelin, Carmarthen, Wales, SA33 5ND, UK
www.crownhouse.co.uk

and

Crown House Publishing Company LLC
PO Box 2223, Williston, VT 05495, USA
www.crownhousepublishing.com

First published 2014. Reprinted 2014, 2015, 2017.

British Library of Cataloguing-in-Publication Data
A catalogue entry for this book is available from the British Library.

Print ISBN 978-184590798-3
Mobi ISBN 978-184590832-4
ePub ISBN 978-184590833-1
ePDF ISBN 978-184590834-8

LCCN 2011940628

Transferred to digital printing 2020

Quotes from Ofsted documents used in this publication have been
approved under an Open Government Licence. Please visit
www.nationalarchives.gov.uk/doc/open-government-licence/

To my brother, James Davies, an incredible man

Acknowledgements

Beverley Randell, Caroline Lenton and all of the Crown House team for their expertise and patience. Thank you to all of the fabulous middle leaders I have met on my travels for inspiring me to write this book.

Contents

Introduction

How to be an Amazing Middle Leader in Schools

How do you find time to inspire others in the busy day-to-day running of a school? How can you learn to delegate and develop staff, rather than just 'dumping' tasks on them? Is it a leadership or management task? Today the myriad of skills needed to be an amazing middle leader in schools can seem mind boggling. What's more, middle leaders are taking up the leadership reins with fewer years of experience than ever before. Recently, when training middle leaders in London, several commented that they were just out of their first year of teaching and were now expected to lead and inspire others! It can seem like a very tall order indeed.

Here's the good news: whether you are new to the role, or are more experienced and aspiring to become a leader, leadership skills *can* be taught. You might not have ten years' leadership experience under your belt, but understanding the important tips, techniques and tools for improving your leadership skills are right at your fingertips.

We've all had some experience of leadership: being led or managed by others. Some of us will have been lucky enough to have experienced the transformational power of the gifted leader; the head teacher or business leader who inspired us to give our best, who communicated their vision for their organisation and, most importantly, had the skills to translate that into reality. When you meet leaders like this the effect they have on everybody in an organisation is immense. Some of their skills appear obvious – clarity of vision, great communication skills and an analytical approach – but they also have other, less obvious skills. These include the way they empower others, deal with change, manage conflict and improve staff motivation and morale.

Some of us have been underwhelmed by the leaders we have worked with. Unfortunately the besieged, dictatorial or just plain ineffective leader is still a reality in some schools, although with increasing accountability their existence is likely to be much shorter lived than in previous years. Many leaders fall somewhere in the spectrum between outstanding and incompetent. Many of us, if truthful, admit that we have real strength and insight in some areas, but lack skill or confidence in others. It is important that we are willing to hold up a mirror to our skills and think about what we can do well and what we need to work on in order to improve ourselves, our staff and move our organisations forward.

I've trained hundreds of middle leaders in the last seven years and have met many more when I've been reviewing schools. This book has partly been written as a result of the emails I receive from the delegates that have attended my Outstanding Middle Leaders training courses, telling me their good news and sometimes requesting further advice on specific issues and examples of good books that they can refer to as a 'practical everyday guide'.

I've also met many excellent middle leaders with strategies, solutions and a heap of helpful ideas; more than can possibly be shoehorned into a couple of days of training. This book has been written so you can learn about the successes of others and avoid the mistakes and missteps that can occur when entering the world of management. It is important to learn from our misjudgements and errors – I've certainly made a few over the years! Making mistakes can be a painful process and reading this book will help you to avoid a few of the common pitfalls. It will also equip you with fantastic tools and helpful tips so that you can strive to be the best middle leader you can, learning from the skills of others, reflecting on examples and getting involved in some of the activities suggested.

Being a successful middle leader in today's world of education is a very exciting proposition – I've been a middle leader in three schools and one large Local Authority. Now I train, coach and assist leaders in schools from across the UK and abroad. I have reviewed departments in many schools, undertaken inspections and met some cracking leaders (and believe me they come in a range of styles and packages!). I've observed how they've inspired, motivated and encouraged other staff so that the pupils in those schools flourish and achieve their very best. Some of their strategies are easily transferrable, others come from a clear personal vision, a high level of interpersonal skills and a relentless enthusiasm to do the best for the pupils in their charge by setting high standards and helping their staff achieve these.

How you use this book is up to you. However, there are a few guiding principles that underpin the way it has been written so understanding them will help you to get the most out of it. As you will realise on your quest to become an outstanding leader, excellence rarely just happens. Learning to lead is a dynamic process. Yes, I know you want some fail-safe tips about leading improvements, sharing your vision and dealing with tricky members of staff and passing Ofsted with flying colours. You can certainly use the book like this. You will gain lots of tips and strategies to use in your leadership role and it will provide food for thought to help you on your way.

However, becoming an amazing leader is a process. Becoming a really amazing leader might involve changing some habits, thinking about things afresh and looking at problems from a completely new angle. With this in mind, at key moments there are **thinking points**. Thinking points let you know that the concept is really rather important and that you might wish to pause and reflect on it. They highlight a key issue connected with leadership and ask you: Is this true in your situation? Do you agree with it? What might be the implications of these actions? In many organisations things run exactly as they always have – sometimes this is a very dangerous thing. Being an amazing leader is having that ability to say, 'Hey – why are we doing it this way?' and to think actively and curiously about the reasons for these behaviours and actions. Thinking points will encourage you to do just that.

Similarly, at the end of some chapters there are **reflection moments**. These encourage you to note down a few things, asking questions such as: What are the three things that have helped you in this chapter? What has caused you to think? What might you want to try in your meetings or your planning? It also encourages you to record a couple of targets related to this area. As research has shown, writing down our intentions is a key way of ensuring that they happen. It provides not only a written reminder, but a commitment to try out and trial some new techniques or ideas. An amazing leader is never afraid to take a risk and try out something new. It's up to you to make the effort to try them and evaluate them, and if they work (remember, not everything works first time – you might need to persevere) you can add them to your leadership repertoire. There is sufficient space in each section of the book for you to write these directly onto the page, but you might like to buy a small notebook and keep your intentions private. This also gives you the opportunity to review chapters as your experience grows as a leader and you can reflect upon your previous answers. Either way, I would urge you to jot down your views.

Feel free to dip into the book and read the chapters you need most. If you feel that an aspect of your leadership needs a boost in a particular area, feel free to start there. Each section makes sense on its own and has been written as a complete unit. Individual chapters also make good INSET material or are helpful for you to look at in detail as a way of improving your practice.

However, since this book is designed to take you on a journey, you will benefit most if you read it from start to finish. Section I looks at the aims, aspirations and skills of an amazing leader; Section II moves on to the practicalities of everyday management tasks, team building and ensuring your vision is shared; Section III looks at the important area of strategic planning and self-evaluation skills; Section IV tackles some of the concerns of leaders about how they will be viewed by Ofsted and what they need to know about this (although following the advice in the whole book will really help you prepare to face scrutiny). The book concludes with a chapter that considers some of the challenges that middle leaders face, as well as looking at how to deal with senior management team (SMT), school governors and external consultants.

This book is the result of visiting hundreds of schools and meeting thousands of middle leaders. A good leader is open-minded and willing to listen to others, so try out some of the techniques and ideas and let me know what works for you – or if you have an even better way of achieving amazing results then let me know! I am always keen to know about the tips and techniques that help you along the way. Like the pupils we teach, we are still developing and learning from our experiences and it is this openness that will set each of us on the right track to become an amazing middle leader.

So, let's get cracking!

Section I

The Skills of an Amazing Middle Leader

Chapter 1

Why We Need to Develop the Skills of an Amazing Middle Leader

So you are a middle leader – congratulations! Now you've decided that you want to be an *amazing* middle leader, let's look at how you can develop your skills to become exceptional. We'll begin with motivation.

People decide to become middle leaders for a whole host of reasons. Some know, right from the start of their teaching career, that the management path is right for them. They are not just interested in being the best Maths teacher they can possibly be, they desire to shape the mathematical experience for *all* the pupils in the school by becoming a curriculum leader. For these individuals, leadership is about seeking and shaping the opportunities of those around them; both the pupils and other teachers. In some cases, their leadership skills are obvious; they have a clear purpose and a relentless drive for leading improvements. Even from their teacher training days their ability to innovate and to inspire others was obvious.

Others are more reluctant leaders, perhaps realising that others in the school are looking to them for guidance, realising that over time they have developed some skills that could be used to encourage and inspire others, almost by osmosis. For some, their leadership skills sneak up on them.

A friend often protested that she didn't want to become a school leader but recently became a cracking deputy head teacher. However, this only happened when she met some external candidates being interviewed for the position and realised, 'Actually, I could do that and I think I'd probably do a much better job!' In her case, her confidence was increased by comparing herself to others in the role.

Are great leaders born — not made?

Some people do appear 'born to lead', but others feel that they have had leadership thrust upon them through circumstance, perhaps by being the only subject specialist in the school, or through the sudden ill health or misfortune of others. Some observe other 'would-be leaders' and realise that they could do the job just as well, if not better than those around them. It doesn't matter *how* you decided to become a leader, what matters is that you did and that while you are leading you seek and strive to become the best leader you possibly can. It sounds relatively straightforward, doesn't it?

I have met a huge range of middle leaders in my role as an adviser, but when I first started on the leadership road in school I felt uncertain and unsure about my role. I had been promoted because an observant Ofsted inspector believed I could teach the much sought after 'outstanding lesson'. I was marked as having management potential. Teaching great lessons is an important aspect of a subject leader, not least because you should be a role model to others; however, there is much more to it than that. Being an outstanding teacher didn't mean that I knew how to set or share a vision, deal with budgets or resolve difficult issues with staff and pupils. These were all important challenges to overcome.

I was lucky in some respects as when I started on the leadership path it was common to 'shadow' and unofficially help out, working alongside more experienced leaders (in those days, without any extra pay), rather than just gaining a quick promotion, as is more often the case now. The advantages to this rather old-fashioned approach are that it was possible to observe and reflect upon the leadership skills of others, and to trial things without having the actual weight of accountability. My head of department was extremely effective (he achieved a great deal), charismatic (he managed to keep us all 'on side' and got us working well for him), and he was extremely well organised and clear sighted (which impressed us and made sure that he actually got the things done he intended to). These aren't all characteristics that come naturally to all of us; however, observing those around us who are successful and effective is one way of helping us see what skills we value. It also helps us to see what strategies these successful people employ to get things done (and of course, to make sure that they are getting the right things done!). Hopefully in your school you will have some examples of excellent leadership to emulate and aspire to, but if you don't then this book will guide you through scenarios and examples for you to reflect on.

Do you need to be an expert about everything?

Developing the skills of an amazing middle leader takes time. It takes effort and ability to have a clear vision about the direction in which you want to take your team and to ensure that you take them on the journey with you. It is all very well rallying the troops, but it takes honesty and integrity to reflect on your own skills, and to consider your own achievements, future possibilities and current limitations. A good leader is not afraid to hold up a mirror to themselves – being honest about their own shortcomings is important. This is so they can be rectified and developed over time, making them a better leader. It does take confidence to be able to do this and to admit that no, you don't actually know everything or have all of the answers – at least, not yet – but you are going to do your best to fill those gaps in your knowledge and expertise so that you and your team continue to make great progress.

Can you do it better?

A good leader realises that along with not having all of the answers all of the time, there is often a better way of doing something. The curriculum and the world of education (both through technology and through politics) means that teachers' jobs are ever changing. A good leader needs to be prepared and flexible enough not only to change with it, but to see the opportunities and obstacles and lead their team over them, reshaping and changing direction as necessary. It takes a good pinch of courage to admit that we don't know everything, even if we have been teaching and leading others a long time, and to be willing and prepared to look at things through fresh eyes.

How long should you have been teaching before you are 'leadership ready'?

People often ask me if there is a length of time they need to have served to become an effective leader. I've met heads of department who have been teaching for twenty-five years who have been innovative and inspirational. I've met some leaders who've only been teaching a couple of years and are highly effective too. Sometimes more so than more 'experienced hands'. They know that because of their obvious inexperience they need to think carefully and really consider their actions and not be afraid to ask others for good advice. It is about having a leadership mindset and following through with the correct actions, aspiring to be the best leader you possibly can for your pupils and team; but it's also being alert to the fact that there might be much better ways of doing things and, if there are, being keen to ferret them out.

Never be complacent!

Complacency is the death of good leadership. I was painfully reminded of this when I was an adviser for a Local Authority. One of my least popular tasks was, in the early weeks of September, visiting the schools who had failed to meet their targets (advisers, after all, are held accountable for the results of schools in their patch). I remember visiting one department where, for a couple of years running, the GCSE results had been in a steady decline. I quizzed the head of department and she shrugged and repeated with hands held aloft that 'we've done what we can ... we're not sure what had happened (again!), and of course, we'll continue to do the best we can this year'. I made my way back to my car with a heavy heart, knowing that without external intervention it was unlikely there would be any real improvement and I would have some difficult follow-up conversations in the following months.

I set off to visit the last school that had also suffered a dip in results that year. I was prepared to be much gentler with the head of department since she was new to the school, and hadn't even been around when the pupils had sat their exams. I didn't really expect much of a response to the question: 'What do you think happened to explain these results?' but I was exceptionally impressed when the head of department gave me her clearly thought-out ideas *and* told me what steps she had already taken to improve things. Not satisfied with the evidence of underachievement, she had scrutinised some of the papers that had been returned with her team (these were the heady days of the SATs papers) and she saw there was evidence that some had been under marked so she sent these back for a re-mark. She also noted that there were some weaknesses in the pupils' approaches to one of the questions, so in consultation with her second in department she made plans to amend some schemes of work to tackle these skills more explicitly. She had produced a very brief action plan with not only intended actions, but also dates and evidence, and talked me through it. She then explained that these were the *only* immediate actions that she was going to take, because if she changed too much in one area the balance of the curriculum would shift and pupils would do less well on other important areas. This was another wise statement; we all know what can happen when we go overboard in one area – it creates an imbalance in the curriculum which creates a different problem for us later on!

Although only a new leader, she had already demonstrated much better leadership skills than the much more experienced head of department who had been 'leading' in the other school for the past fifteen years. It was no surprise when the new head of department's team rapidly improved its results; and as for the other school, well that's a different story.

So as an amazing leader we have to be willing to think and sometimes rethink the way we go about doing things, whether that is planning to raise achievement, dealing with staff members or deciding how best to spend the budget. What is clear about exceptional leaders is that they are always aware that there might be a better way of doing things and that they still have plenty to learn about teaching, getting the best out of their team members and, ultimately, themselves as leaders.

Chapter 2

Examining the 5 As
of Amazing Leadership

In defining the essence of an amazing leader, I find it helps to think about the five As of middle leadership: Aspiration, Authenticity, Analytical skills, Approachability and Adaptability. These reflect the key skills that a great leader has in abundance. Developing and working on these skills will take time and commitment, as well as real honesty to think about the areas in which you excel and those where you might be lacking. It is important to consider what you can do to bolster these areas. You will doubtless feel that some of these come very naturally to you, but the ones you feel less confident in are probably the best to start with.

1. Aspiration

A good leader needs to have very clear aspirations for their pupils and their team. Arguably the most important job we do as a leader is to encourage *all* pupils to aim high and achieve their full potential. This can only happen if we ensure that these high aspirations are shared and made possible by the team we lead, including not only teachers but teaching assistants and other support staff. Being aspirational means that a team leader sees the potential in *all* of the pupils and staff in the school. They strive to make sure that all pupils receive the opportunity to gain the very best education they can, so they enjoy and achieve in that area – whether it is secondary school French or literacy skills in Year 2. This is the top quality that leaders need to make them amazing. Of course, it needs to be tempered with some softer people skills too – a 100% aspirational middle leader with no other attributes sounds like a very scary proposition, but it is vitally important that leaders seek the highest standards possible and ensure that these are shared and embedded across the team.

I travel across the country visiting many schools and it quickly becomes apparent whether the middle leaders in a school have high aspirations for their subject areas or not. Only last month, I visited a sixth form college in a deprived area of outer London. As they showed me around, one middle leader highlighted students' success stories displayed on the wall and showed off the newest learning resources, explaining that because most of the students came from a deprived background where most parents had not stayed on at school beyond 16, their primary job at the college was to inspire the students to take their studies seriously. Their key role was to encourage them to continue to university and college, arranging visits, extra activities and motivational outside speakers, because, as he put it, 'They don't get much encouragement at home, so it is our job to inspire them and make sure they achieve and see what the wider world has to offer.' This was a place of learning that had the highest expectations for *all* of their students.

There was no hiding behind excuses about a pupil's background as being a reason to accept failure or a lack of achievement. The air of aspiration was almost tangible, and this was translated into specific actions with clear outcomes, rather than a vague hope that pupils would somehow just achieve. This contrasts with some places, where 'pupil deprivation', 'turbulent pupil population' and 'poor pupil behaviour' are trotted out as excuses for not expecting the best and getting the best out of students.

Are aspirations just hopes?

Of course, 'aspirations' must not be hollow words or empty promises – the high aspirations of a head of department must be backed up by solid actions, clear priorities and solid outcomes, otherwise it's just a smoky illusion. However, it is important to start with very clear aspirations for the pupils in your charge, your team and, of course, yourself as a leader and teacher.

Ofsted commonly ask heads of departments what their most important job is as a middle leader. They often receive the answer that it is to 'support their team' and 'ensure that the teachers in their team are able to teach great lessons' and that 'they have the resources and guidance to allow them to do this well'. However, this is not the right answer. Although these things are important, the most important role of the middle leader is to ensure that students *achieve* their potential; that they learn very well in lessons and that they enjoy learning. This needs to be the primary focus. If you can get this right then everything else should follow. The first question a middle leader should ask is not, 'What would makes Ms Jones' teaching easier/better/more engaging?' but, 'What do the pupils need to learn well and make great progress?' and then, 'What needs to happen to make this possible?' It is only a slight difference, but an important one.

Having high aspirations sounds straightforward, but it is not without issues. You might have people in your team who don't share your high aspirations: the teachers who prefer being 'okay' rather than attempting to be 'outstanding', or those who would rather argue that Dan is a potential D grade than stick their neck out and press him and themselves to achieve a C grade. Aspiration isn't just having the vague hope that things will be better – it means putting strategies into place so that positive and beneficial changes will and do take place. We will delve into this in more detail throughout the book.

Making aspirations into clear visions

It is important to have a clear vision about your department. To have clear aims relating to your vision of your department, it is worth thinking: if I had the best Science department/sixth form/Early Years setting, then what would it look like? What would be happening? How would pupils be learning? What would they be doing in lessons? How would teachers be teaching? What extra-curricular enrichment might there be? What would I want pupils saying about Science in school? This should give you a very clear aspirational vision – then you need to think about where you currently are and what you could do to make this vision a reality.

Having aspirations is important, whether that's aspiring for your pupils to achieve their very best, for 10% more to take Spanish at GCSE or for there to be a rich diet of extra-curricular events. Or as one new head of department told me, 'Pupils in this school have five lessons a day – I want them to come to English knowing that they will have their *best* lesson of the day.

This is what governs all my actions.' It is a pretty high aspiration, but not a bad one to have, particularly if it helps you drive forward improvements.

Read on for ideas.

2.   Authenticity

Having high aspirations for your pupils and staff is really important, but it needs to be firmly aligned with being authentic as a leader. Being authentic is about having the right motivations. It is about being genuine. It is about being honest. Authentic leaders are those that do the right thing, in the right way, for the right reasons. It can appear quite difficult discussing authenticity, but if you have ever met someone who is not authentic as a leader then you will know why I feel the need to mention it here and why it needs to be the bedrock underpinning all you do.

The authentic leader has a genuine desire to do the best for their pupils and staff. They are driven by the desire to improve things for the pupils and staff in their charge. Of course, you might have some personal ambition too. You may wish to progress to becoming an assistant or deputy head in a few years and this is no bad thing, as long as you remain authentic to your primary purpose: to improve the teaching and learning for the pupils in your care and to guide and assist your team in doing so.

Of course, you will want to succeed and have a good track record of success. It needs to be clear that improvements have happened, and you will, of course, add to your CV as a side effect of your success! However, a dynamic head of department spoke to me recently about her work as head of MFL in a school which had a turbulent past, coming out of

Special Measures. She said, 'My most important job is to make sure that MFL continues to improve, that pupils enjoy lessons and achieve their target grades. I need to keep consistency in my team and secure good teaching, keeping my team following in the same direction, developing them as teachers so that *we* become an outstanding department.' When asked about her own personal ambition, she was honest: 'I do have some personal ambitions (she saw herself as an assistant head teacher in a few years); however, that is something very separate to my role as a head of department. I need to ensure that all changes are embedded and that things are deeply improved – leading this department isn't just a quick route up the career ladder. It needs to be sustainable, and the things that I have put into place (embedding Assessment for Learning (AfL) strategies, interactive teaching and learning techniques, using ICT in the classroom) need to continue, work well and be refined.'

This is authentic leadership. She is keen to help her staff become better and ensures that she skills them up, so that when she is ready for promotion the good work and rationale for improvements don't just slide and collapse without her, they will continue.

Mr or Mrs Fake-It!

We have all experienced somebody more senior in school or wider life being inauthentic as a leader or person in power. When having drinks at the House of Commons I was interested to hear from some of the politicians milling around about how they saw their role. Without exception, the handful I spoke to were super keen to boast about their power, their influence and the way they could quickly change things. It was clear their driving force was the love of power and the desire for other people to see them as very important. They were out to impress. What was completely missing in all of their conversations about the changes they were planning to drive through was why they thought it needed to be done and, most importantly, how it was intended to change the lives of everyday people for the better. Having the power to improve people's lives is fantastic, but power as a pure ego trip and leadership without authenticity of purpose is repugnant.

When we are leading projects in schools we need to be wary of this. Occasionally we observe a member of the leadership team starting a new initiative in schools. This is great if it addresses a real need for our pupils and staff (that's a crucial part of their job) but occasionally it appears that it is just a ticket to the next promotion or a way of completing an important part of a leadership qualification, rather than ensuring a school's continual improvement by addressing something important, of benefit to the children and staff.

Great leaders learn from mistakes – and make 'em!

Being authentic as a leader is also about being honest. I have always respected and worked very hard for those leaders who were genuine. I worked for one head of department who was highly organised and very innovative; occasionally he would make a mistake or try out a pilot project and it would go wrong. He would always admit this and explain, and be quick to apologise if his error had inconvenienced you. I admired this leader as he wasn't afraid to show his fallibility (luckily his errors were very few) and he learnt from his mistakes, never making the same one twice. I appreciated the fact that before we all had to undertake the latest 'initiative', he would have trialled it out. This helped us as a department to avoid the common pitfalls that often occur with any change. Realising that he was not putting himself up there as an infallible leader also created a culture in the department where it was alright to take risks with your teaching (if it went wrong nobody would think any less of you and, who knows, you might do something exceptional!). It also encouraged a free exchange of creative ideas across the team. It was a refreshing place to work.

On the other hand, working for leaders who are capricious, underhand, play politics and will never ever admit that they have made a mistake (when you know they have) leads to an air of distrust and stifles innovation. We need to know that those who lead us have our best interests at heart and that if they make a mistake are big enough to hold their hands up and say, 'Let's learn from this and do better next time.'

If leaders are inauthentic, teams begin to suspect and doubt them; conversations are too guarded. If people are unable to make mistakes then they fail to learn. One of the most authentic and successful heads of department I know has a simple policy; she says, 'I refuse to get involved in politics. If things go wrong, I say, "What can we do to fix it?" I am not about blame.' Hers is a happy, successful department in an outstanding school because she lives her philosophy every day in the way she interacts with pupils and staff.

3. Analytical

A good leader needs to be analytical. Analytical leaders are able to take an overview of a situation and are able to think about why things might be the way they are and what might make them better. An analytical leader asks a lot of questions of other people and themselves. They don't presume to know all of the answers, but they have good mechanisms to find things out. The analytical leader uses reason, hard facts and data to support their views. They may have a hunch that something might work or that it's a good idea, but they make decisions after looking at the right facts.

Being analytical is about asking the right questions, finding out the important things and then using this information to lead improvements. It is about constantly evaluating and reflecting on things that have gone well and thinking about what things could have gone better: learning from the past in terms of successes and mistakes. It is about being reflective, thinking and reviewing. This all sounds quite straight-forward, but it can be very hard in the day-to-day running of school to keep those analytical skills fresh at the forefront of your mind.

One of the main barriers to being analytical is when you have been in the post for a long while (anything over eighteen months counts here). We all know the experience of getting a new job. In the first few weeks we question everything we do: Why do we do teach x topic first? Why are meetings always on a Tuesday? Why do we do assessments then? After a while these decisions become part of the fabric of the school and part of the 'way we do things around here'. This can often be very dangerous. We need to keep questioning why we do things the way we are doing them – if the answer is because it is effective because the evidence, the results and the children tell us so, then this is fine.

If, however, we fall back on the comment: 'We do it because we've always done it this way,' then this can be indicative of lazy thinking and needs challenging. Once I ran some whole school training on 'Teaching Outstanding Lessons' on the last day of the Christmas term; it was a very long morning session which ended with the staff Christmas lunch. It was clear that many of the teachers' minds were more focused on the imminent Christmas break and feast of turkey awaiting them than the important issues that the training was raising; however, I rallied them and we had a successful morning. I noted that on the evaluation forms many staff had commented that the training had been great but they would have loved a whole day at a time of year when they weren't exhausted and so desperate for their Christmas break.

As the deputy head congratulated me on a successful event, I raised my thoughts with her and shared the evaluations. Wouldn't the training have been even better if it had been at the start of the January term? Or if there had been time to allow staff a session to reflect on the training and make an action plan for the future? Might this be a good plan for future training? The deputy head explained that it was 'tradition that the last day of the Christmas term was used for training, before their turkey trimmings Christmas lunch' and admitted that there were issues with this – but of course, it was a long-standing tradition and would continue – and did I want to train them next Christmas?

As a leader, we need to make ourselves open to feedback; to reflect on what has gone well and what could be better. When we hear the words, 'It is because we've always done it this way,' we need to be alert to the fact that there might be lazy thinking and lazy leadership at play and be prepared to challenge it! After all, we wouldn't want to live up to Bertrand

Russell's observation: 'Many people would rather die than think. In fact they do.' Being a leader is about being a critical and astute thinker and using these skills to lead improvements.

Middle leaders don't receive much (read enough!) non-contact time to be analytical and to reflect. This is where, in many schools, a heavy teaching load, dealing with emergencies and just the hurly-burly of an everyday busy school means that these crucial skills get neglected. If head teachers really want to improve the exam success of key subjects then they need to think about giving much more non-contact time to heads of department to allow them to use this strategic skill. It might be radical to suggest reversing the non-contact frees of assistant head teachers and heads of department in key subjects but this would help. Middle leaders need *more* time to oversee what is happening and to ensure the quality control of what is going on, to allow them not only to identify issues but also to lead changes. Many assistant head teachers could manage with much less (but of course they don't get this since they design the timetables!).

Being analytical is a crucial skill – it helps us prioritise and focus on what's important (rather than just urgent), and lead our teams on to further success. One wise head teacher said to me early in my leadership career, 'It is important not to be bogged down in the everyday, all day, in too fine detail. You need to look up and out at your department from the bird's eye view to see the strengths, the weaknesses and where you need to take it next.' We will be looking at skills for doing this in further chapters.

4. Approachable

Are you approachable? Do staff ask you things? Do they check things through with you? Are you offered a biscuit at breaktime? Are you around at lunchtime? It is very important to be seen as approachable by your staff. This is not the same thing as you *thinking* that you are approachable. It is important as a middle leader to be available to your staff. By this I don't mean 24/7, but I mean being around regularly, so that they can run ideas by you, have a friendly chat and raise any concerns or generate some good ideas with you on an informal basis, as well as through the regular meeting cycle.

Approachability is important for many reasons and there doesn't need to be just one way of achieving this. If you aren't approachable enough to staff, if you are too scary/unavailable/distant then several things might happen. If staff only have the opportunity to ask you questions or have brief exchanges between lessons or in the formality of a meeting then they might stop doing so. This might mean that they start going 'maverick' and do their own thing, which could involve some marvellous innovations (which you won't know about) or end up with them teaching the wrong topic/exam requirements (which can have terrible repercussions). They might not do things that you expect them to because they aren't sure of the requirements, or they could start going over your head: 'You weren't around to ask, so I went to Pam (the deputy head) instead.'

All of these things are potentially undermining and can cause a lack of consistency in your team. So you do need to be approachable and available.

Always on call?

There is the danger of going to the other extent too. Being too available can lead to constant interruptions to your lessons and your day can be frustrating as you never get things done for yourself. It is difficult to crunch data if Ian is always popping in every five minutes asking you for ideas for teaching Year 5 Geography/dealing with Keisha/finding the book cupboard key. A good middle leader often decides which lunchtimes or breaktimes they will be around for staff, either in the working area or the classroom, and let it be known. The end of the school day is often a good time to be available to staff as many people are more relaxed and have time to talk, although if you have other commitments and need to get home promptly on a regular basis then you need to make yourself more available within the school day and also be aware of your team's working patterns and commitments outside school.

Sometimes staff will expect you to deal with things and help them when it just isn't an appropriate moment for you – you are just about to teach a class or you are in the middle of a tricky piece of work. I have found a phrase quite useful for dealing with these interruptions If someone asks if you have five minutes but you really haven't, and you can see it isn't a health and safety emergency that demands your immediate attention, say: 'I am a bit busy now, but I am happy to talk to you about it properly next lesson/lunchtime/end of school.' This means that you don't feel frustrated and ambushed by their requests, but you have acknowledged them and agreed to give them quality time later. The other advantage to this approach is if they are just being lazy and trying to get you to do/find/sort something out for them which they could really do themselves, they will often resolve it themselves. However, if it is a more important issue then you are giving them the time to deal with it later and they will appreciate this.

5. Adaptable

Last, but by no means least, is the ability to be adaptable. This is a critical skill for a great leader. Running a team as a middle leader needs a good deal of flexibility of thought. You don't always know what is going to happen next, and this is particularly true if you are a head of year or do a lot of pastoral work. Running a large team throws up many issues: staff might be absent, issues might flare up with pupils, parents might suddenly arrive. You need to be able to quickly decide how to deal with these: which things can be left and what the appropriate actions to take are.

Flexibility of thought and attitude is also very important in the ever changing world of education and leadership. If we are too rigid or too fixed in our views, if we are not able to adapt and change our ideas to meet the current circumstances, then there is a real danger we can get stressed and snap.

Adaptability is also important in the classroom. When you are a leader the quality of the lessons you teach are still very important. You need to be able to consistently teach good lessons. This is important for a myriad of reasons – from the fact that all pupils need great lessons, to the need for you to be a good role model for the rest of the department. A good leader also needs to be a very good classroom teacher and to be prepared to try out and adapt new techniques, particularly if they are trying to encourage other staff to try these strategies in their classes.

However, what is different as a leader is that you no longer have as much time to spend planning your lessons. As a newly qualified teacher (NQT), your only real responsibility would have been planning and marking and you could afford to lavish hours of care on this. Now you still need to be able to deliver good lessons, but your time for planning them has shrunk drastically. This is why I would urge all 'would be' leaders to ensure that they have the skills of a good teacher already secured before taking on a leadership role. You need to be able to draw on 'what works', your knowledge of how to plan interesting and engaging lessons that help the pupils' progress, and to be able to do this fairly quickly because you will have a list of other management tasks to do. The quality of adaptability is important here as a good teacher can quickly adapt ideas from other lessons, get ideas from online resources and, if the lesson they have planned appears to be faltering, they will be ready to amend it and adapt it during the lesson.

We do need to be really good teachers and role models for our staff. We need to be able to adapt from our role as a good PE teacher to our role in managing behaviour in our department area, or looking at the achievement of *all* Year 10 students, or dealing with a staffing problem in our History department. The ability to deal with one thing and then change and deal with someone or something else is an important skill.

One thing that is always a constant in education is that it is changing, whether it is changing exam board specifications, government expectations, head teacher demands on us or just the different types of pupils in our school or new staff members joining us. It is about trying to predict and limit the negative implications of possible changes so that we are ready for them, and can incorporate them into our teams without too much difficulty. Not being sufficiently adaptable results in additional stress for us and our teams. Adaptable leaders are adept at meeting changes or handling difficult circumstances with confidence because they can draw on their past successes to help them. They don't despair when they are told that they have got two new students to place, the book order has been delayed or that the head teacher wants some suggestions for spending some extra funding to raise achievement. They have the ability and the creativity to deal with the unexpected, and the support of their team to help them do so.

Reflection moment

So how are your five As? Which of the characteristics do you think you possess the most? Make a quick note of these now. Which areas do you think you could do with a little more enhancement in? Take the following light-hearted assessment which will help you identify some of your areas of strength and give you some possible areas of improvement. If you are after a more objective view then get a colleague who knows you well to complete this with you and who will be able to advise you if they think that you are really giving honest answers. For each question, mark the answer that is most like you and then also indicate the answer that is least like you.

Chapter 3

Questionnaire: What is Your Core A Leadership Strength?

The following questionnaire is designed to help you understand how your responses to situations and attitudes match the five As. For each question, try to imagine the situation that is being described and choose the answer that would be your most frequent response.

---

1. **Pupil interviews have identified that some pupils do not enjoy the Year 7 lessons based on your schemes of work. The criticism is that they are boring and repeat some work they did in Year 6.**

a. You see this as an excellent opportunity to revamp the whole of Key Stage 3. You have got lots of ideas for adding challenge. You will organise meetings with the primary feeder schools to ensure that this will be appropriate.
b. You are very disappointed with this as you wanted to ensure challenge. You have taken this to heart and feel quite crushed by this response.
c. You will analyse the questionnaire in more detail to find out exactly what pupils didn't like and see if this is common across the year. Then you plan to drill down into what exactly pupils do at primary school and how you can build on this.

d.   You aren't surprised by this because some pupils had already told you this. You plan to discuss this issue at a future department meeting to see what suggestions your team can make for improvements.

e.   You think that one of the local secondary schools has overcome a similar transition issue. You are thinking about getting in contact with them to find out how they have resolved it before you start tackling it yourself.

2.   If someone new was joining your team, a current staff member is most likely to say to them:

a.   Chris has high standards and accepts nothing but the best efforts from pupils and staff. We achieve great things – but it's hard work!

b.   Chris really cares about what she is doing and she is really passionate about the pupils/French/the school.

c.   Chris is perceptive; she can organise you and quantify you from fifty feet. If you want to do something, she'll say 'show me the evidence'.

d.   Chris is great – she's always got good ideas but she really includes everyone; there's lots of sharing in the team. It's a friendly place.

e.   Chris always finds solutions – she's a really creative thinker. She's just managed to get us some great new resources for next to nothing!

3.   You are most excited to be a middle leader because:

a.   You want to raise results and really make a difference to the experience of pupils. You want them to love Maths and achieve the highest grades.

b.   You know that you are a great teacher, but in leading a team you can share your experience, raise the expertise of others and make a big difference.

   c.   You love finding out why things are the way they are, analysing them and seeing what makes the difference – you are nifty with a spreadsheet too.

   d.   You like working in a team and getting the best out of people.

   e.   You love the variety of the role. One minute you are teaching, then coaching others, planning for improvements and deciding on new resources – there's never a dull moment.

4.   Your mantra for leadership is:

   a.   You need to aim high: less than the best isn't good enough!

   b.   I will be the change I want to see in others.

   c.   Show me the data!

   d.   There's no 'i' in team leader.

   e.   So it doesn't work – I've got another idea!

5.   In a team meeting you are most likely to be heard saying:

   a.   The best way to raise results is …

   b.   The best thing for the pupils is for …

   c.   The data suggests …

   d.   My NQT has had a really brilliant idea that I think we should consider.

   e.   There are three different ways of approaching this problem.

6.   You are most likely to have conflict with other staff when:

   a.   You think they are not pulling their weight and are not getting the best out of the pupils.

   b.   You feel that they are out for themselves and not the good of the school.

c.   You have spotted something that they are not doing as well as they could be and you point this out.

d.   You have been too friendly with them socially and struggle when you need to tell them about their marking/time keeping, etc.

e.   You fail to explain your thoughts to them clearly enough. They don't understand the reasons behind your actions.

7.   **When you are interviewing an NQT you are most impressed by those that:**

a.   Have excellent qualifications and look like they are experts.

b.   Show that they have a passion for teaching and connect well with pupils.

c.   Are aware of their weaknesses and strengths and know what they need to do to improve.

d.   Look like they are friendly, will fit in with the team well and have a great personality.

e.   Have a lot of different skills and look like they will be flexible with what they can offer.

8.   **When people visit your area for the first time they are most impressed by:**

a.   The displays showing work at different levels and the fact that all pupils know exactly what they are aiming for and how to get there.

b.   The warm atmosphere and the sense of excitement about learning.

c.   The fact that you are very aware of the department's strengths and can whip out an action plan.

d.   The fact that the team seem to be happy, everybody is around at breaktime and there are always biscuits and cake on offer.

e. You are innovative and are skilled at dealing with difficult issues.

9. **In a department meeting you are most likely to be concerned about:**

a. Target grades and the results of the Mocks, highlighting underachievers.
b. Focusing on what you think is the biggest issue at the moment.
c. Showing the team the results of the latest pupil voice.
d. Ensuring that everybody has a say and feels valued.
e. Ensuring that you get time to talk about the latest developments in your area.

10. **If you met a pupil in Tesco in ten years' time, you would be most pleased to hear them say:**

a. Because of you I achieved a C grade. It helped me get my dream job.
b. I knew you always believed in me!
c. I loved the way that when you marked my work you knew exactly what I needed to do to make it better.
d. I always felt I could talk to you and could ask you for help.
e. I like the fact that you did so many different things with our year group; I remember …

11. **One thing you need to be careful about is:**

a. Driving yourself and your team too hard in the quest for ever greater achievement.
b. Presuming that everybody shares your ideal when in fact they don't. Some people are motivated by different things.
c. Over analysing things so you don't actually take any action.

d. Allowing yourself to be too friendly with staff so that you can't talk to them about issues that need addressing.

e. Knowing that your quick thinking can always get you out of trouble, so you don't plan as carefully as you should.

Tot up the marks for each question. You will see that your answers broadly relate to the five different As. Answer A = Aspirational, B = Authentic, C = Analytical, D = Approachable, E = Adaptable.

Reflection moment

Have a look at your results. Which area came up with the highest number of marks? This is your most dominant A. If you have a dominant letter, flip back and reread the description of that skill. It is clearly an important skill to have, but it is important to foster all of the As to be an exceptional leader. If there is a letter that you did not select for any answer, then it is worth reading that description again to see if you might need some enhancement in that area. There isn't a right or wrong answer for these questions, but if you repeatedly get one response it might be worth thinking about what you can learn from the other A sections. Use the description of this A to give you some pointers about addressing the balance. Remember, it is important to develop a range of skills so you can call on them when it is most appropriate and become a really amazing middle leader.

Leading a Team and Getting the Right Things Done!

Chapter 4

What's the Difference Between Leadership and Management?

What is the difference between leadership and management? This is the classic interview question for middle leaders. Why do many schools now call their teams the senior *leadership* team, rather than the senior *management* team? Have managers morphed into the new leaders? And does it really matter what you are called?

Personally, I don't really think it matters what you are called, but what does matter is how you see your role, and, most importantly, what you actually do and what you achieve for the pupils in your school. Years ago heads of department, year heads, year coordinators (call them what you will) appeared to focus very much on the management side of things: ordering resources, books, arranging things, sorting them out. It was said that a manager was somebody 'who got things done'. They were known for their efficient tick lists and for being a 'completer/finisher'. You could trust a manager with getting things ordered, filed, sorted and organised. Leadership, well that was something else.

Managers are people who are efficient, who follow directions, who ensure if you are going on holiday that everything is securely and carefully packed, all ticked off on an Edexcel spreadsheet; they've got the map, they've got the tickets and they ensure that everybody's on time and that the car has been serviced and that there's plenty of petrol ...You get the picture. Managers, it seems, are invaluable.

What about leaders? What's their role? What's the difference? Well the manager might have everything carefully packed, but it is the leader who has decided that a trip needs be taken in the first place. They have envisaged what type of trip the family needs, they have weighed up their aspirations and made the best choices from the available budget. They have chosen the destination! Yes, the manager might have everybody strapped in the car with enough clean underpants to last them the fortnight, but it is the leader who has decided that they should all go on holiday; they have a clear idea of what they hope to get out of it and why it is the best destination.

In previous years, the term 'leader' was exclusively reserved for head teachers, rather than deputies or even heads of department. This was because it was thought that only the head teacher could set the direction for their school. After setting the path and having the all-important vision, they would instruct the deputies and then the heads of department about what their route was. It was the job of these middle managers to pack the car, secure the house and make sure that they had made enough sandwiches for the trip! Now, it is still understood that good leadership of a school is reliant on very clear direction and leadership skills from the head teacher; however, all areas of the school, including governors and middle leaders, have a role in shaping and leading – 'distributed leadership' is the buzz phrase.

We want heads of department/heads of year/heads of pastoral not just to be the person who marshals resources, but the one who inspires, sets a clear direction for their team, who leads with the end point in mind, so that their subject or area can flourish under their leadership. Filling the car with petrol is very important and so is ensuring that your staff have the right resources to do their job well, but setting the right course and agreeing on the direction should come first. We want to get to the right place, for the right reason, not just any place.

The current educational climate also reinforces the need for *leadership*, rather than management skills at every level in school. Schools in the UK are evaluated and judged by Ofsted and their evaluation schedule for school inspection increasingly places emphasis on the role of the middle *leader*, as opposed to manager. This isn't designed to be a book about Ofsted, or just how to get a gold star on your inspection – although it will undoubtedly help, this book is about developing the skills of being a great leader and achieving the best for your pupils. However, where relevant and helpful, I will make reference to Ofsted's concerns and link these with effective leadership advice.

The 2013 Ofsted Evaluation Schedule, for example, explains the importance of leadership skills in its choice of vocabulary: 'leaders focus relentlessly on teaching and learning and provide focused professional development for all staff and lead by example. They base their actions on a deep and accurate understanding of the school's performance and of staff and pupils' skills and attributes.' Here not only is the language based more on leadership attributes but also the implications. The manager might sort through and offer staff a choice of different day INSET courses to attend for their professional development, but the leader correctly identifies and analyses what the pupils' and staff's needs actually are and then devises the best continuing professional development (CPD) for them. This may be a one day course, but it might include training groups of teachers at school, setting up coaching cycles or devising other types of CPD. A good leader sees the 'big picture' and the ultimate aim – they don't see running a team just as a set of tasks to complete.

Chapter 5

Starting Points: Where Are We? What's Working? What Could be Better?

Being a leader involves really thinking about the outcome you want and planning strategically to achieve this, rather than just completing daily tasks. I remember, as an inexperienced middle leader, realising that the team did not use as much ICT in their teaching as they might. I arranged for individuals to attend separate, eye-wateringly expensive one-day training events in London and was subsequently surprised when their practice wasn't magically transformed. Although I felt I could tick off 'attend ICT training' on their performance management targets, the actual practice in the classroom hadn't improved. The desired outcome of having all staff being efficient users of ICT to help pupils progress would have been more successfully achieved if I had organised central training for the whole team or had organised a 'buddy system' (whereby staff who were more proficient at ICT taught others). Being a leader is about imagining the desired outcome and ensuring it happens in the best way – not just any way.

Arranging the timetable, buying resources, starting new exam specifications, organising special events, planning interventions for groups of pupils all have aspects of management to them; they need to be well planned and organised. But, first of all, the leader needs a clear rationale as to why they are happening and a clear idea of what they hope to achieve.

You might like to look at Ofsted's criteria for outstanding leadership and management below – it isn't designed as a tick sheet but does provide some of the expectations and actions that are required. We will be addressing these areas throughout the book. It has been accessed from the Ofsted website and some of the key areas most pertinent to middle leaders have been listed. You are advised to review the website as Ofsted regularly makes changes and additions to what is expected from leaders.

- The pursuit of excellence in all of the school's activities is demonstrated by an uncompromising and highly successful drive to strongly improve, or maintain, the highest levels of achievement and personal development for all pupils over a sustained period of time.

- All leaders and managers are highly ambitious for the pupils and lead by example. They base their actions on a deep and accurate understanding of the school's performance, and of staff and pupils' skills and attributes.

- There are excellent policies underpinning practice that ensures that pupils have high levels of literacy, or pupils are making excellent progress in literacy.

- Leaders focus relentlessly on improving teaching and learning and provide focused professional development for all staff, especially those that are newly qualified and at an early stage of their careers. This is underpinned by searching performance management that encourages, challenges and supports teachers' improvement. As a result, teaching is outstanding, or at least consistently good and improving.

- The school's curriculum promotes and sustains a thirst for knowledge and a love of learning. It covers a wide range of subjects and provides opportunities for academic, technical and sporting excellence. It has a very positive impact on all pupils' behaviour and safety, and contributes very well to pupils' academic achievement, their physical wellbeing, and their spiritual, moral, social and cultural development.

- The school's actions have secured improvement in achievement for those supported by the pupil premium, which is rising rapidly, including in English and mathematics.

- The school has highly successful strategies for engaging with parents to the benefit of pupils, including those who find working with the school difficult.

- Staff model professional standards in all of their work and demonstrate high levels of respect and courtesy for pupils and others.[1]

Developing your vision

As a middle leader it is very important to have a clear vision. You need to know what it will look like if your Design and Technology department/Year 1 team/Year 10 tutor team are exceptional. It is important that as the leader you can visualise in detail what it would be like to have the best provision possible (what is being offered to pupils, such as the curriculum) and what the outcomes would be. What would the pupils say, do and achieve if things were really outstanding in your area of the school? How would other teaching team members and non-teaching staff know that

---

[1] Ofsted, *School Inspection Handbook*, 2014, Ref. 120101.

this team was outstanding? What would be the indicators? What would they be doing? How would they feel? What about the senior leadership team and the governors? What sort of outcomes would they be hoping for? What sort of feedback would you be hoping for and expecting from parents and the wider community? How would Ofsted know that they were dealing with an exceptional leader?

This might all seem somewhat overwhelming, until it's broken down. It is important to consider these questions and to think about what you are hoping to achieve before you start leading. In many of our experiences we simply hope to replicate the actions of our predecessor. They ran it this way, so we will. This can be a starting point if we are taking over an already successful team, but we also need to look outwards as well as inwards to continue and further develop our success.

In this section we are going to look at the strategies you should be undertaking to audit where you currently are with your team, and we will discuss the next steps needed for making your vision a success. In doing this we will be looking at your role, but also at how you need to be meeting the needs of the various stakeholders in bringing about success.

Opposite is a familiar diagram that shows the improvement cycle in any organisation. It is useful to remind ourselves that improvements aren't static; we don't just tick them off as a job done. A good leader never says, 'Right, well I've tackled the "Gifted and Talented" issue.' They take action, but this isn't the end. We need to think about where we are, and what we might need to do to improve, not forgetting the importance of reflection and evaluation of the effect of our actions. The good leader will want to reflect on what went well in improving provision for 'Gifted and Talented' pupils, but will also consider whether anything could have been improved and should be adjusted for next time.

What was
the outcome?
What worked
well?

Where are
we now?

What is our
priority?
What will we
do about it?

What are
similar
schools/departments
achieving?

What more
should we
hope to
achieve?

Cycle of improvements

Chapter 6

Where Are We Currently? Talk to the Team

This is a really important question for any leader. Where are we? What is the current state of affairs? What appears to be working? What are our weaknesses as well as our strengths? If you are very familiar with your team and school you may think that you know all of the answers. However, whatever you *think* is the reality (whether good or bad), it is always really important to evaluate the hard evidence.

What if you are a brand new leader? You might be a newcomer to the school, just finding your way around – how can you hope to quickly grasp the situation and make plans for driving things forward? There are several things you need to do. Some of these will produce 'hard' data and some of it much softer.

Talk to the team

Once, at a formal dinner, I met the head of a large police force. I was interested in his job (not least because I had just had my car vandalised and the unsympathetic Wellingborough police operator told me to consider myself very lucky that it still had wheels!).

The head of the force had just moved to a new position hundreds of miles away from his usual patch, taking up the command of thousands of police officers and a huge budget. I was intrigued – how did he decide what to do first in this brand new area? His answer was interesting: one of the things that he found particularly valuable was to speak to the next layer of police officers under him to ask them the following questions individually: What are the three things we do really well in policing in x region? What two things do you think we should do better? What should we do about them? After talking to a number of staff he said he had some real starting points. They had given him clear information about what *they* thought was working well and what their next priorities should be.

Obviously he needed to check these ideas against the hard data of what was actually happening in the area, but this initial approach in tackling a new team has several benefits. It allows you to see what the team *thinks* should be its priority – if this mirrors the actual evidence then it helps you embed your vision, since staff will more likely to *buy in* to an idea if they feel that they have helped generate it. For example, if staff think that independent learning should be their priority and your lesson observations and other evidence also indicate this, then it is a sign that this is probably an important area to tackle.

It is also important to hear what staff already think is working well and what could be better, because it gives them the opportunity to make suggestions and explain any frustrations that might be hindering them from doing the best job possible. When I was researching this book, I asked many leaders and many ordinary teachers what they thought the most important quality was in middle leadership. The main scale teachers mostly spoke about the need for middle leaders to use their talents, take suggestions and involve the main scale teachers in gaining ideas and setting a vision. A teacher I know reinforced this by saying: 'A good leader should not be afraid to take others' thoughts and ideas into consideration, or even to admit that they don't know every-thing and would sometimes need a little help.'

Two of the most off-putting things many main scale staff found about leaders were that they 'thought they knew it all already' or they 'tried to rush in changes too quickly, throwing out the good ideas as well as the bad ones'. If nothing else, taking time to ask staff about what they think are the issues, and what simple changes could make things more effective for the team, means that staff feel consulted, and empowered if their suggestions are acted upon. Let's not forget that the 'everyday' teacher is in the prime pos-ition to know what could be better in their area and we'd be foolish not to at least listen to their ideas.

Although I've been a leader in several organisations, I've done plenty of years as a 'foot soldier' in three schools and several different organisations. What really demotivates you as a member of staff is when you can see what needs to be fixed, but you aren't even asked or listened to when you offer solutions. Middle leaders (and senior leaders) who lis-ten are appreciated, respected and can actually move things forward. Of course, it is crucial to test the evidence that things do need improving, rather than rushing in straight away on your team's say so. Your team members may be spot on and have astutely identified an issue; on the other hand, they could have a misconception or be after changes that wouldn't really address the most important issue – it might make their life easier, but it might not be the best thing for the pupils.

Team leaders who start from the perspective of *first* asking their team what they think the changes should be, then tri-angulating this by checking it against other evidence, have led a number of successful changes. Some of these sound very small, some bigger, but because they were the right change they had a huge impact on the pupils. Successes triggered from discussions with middle leaders include: in

Design and Technology curriculum planning changed so that progression across years was improved, new resources were purchased for MFL and some training in them so that staff could best use the ICT to teach great lessons, a buddying/mentoring system was started in vertical tutor groups to promote better reading skills, department meetings improved to include a 'resource of the week' so that people could learn from each other's good practice and save themselves time in preparing resources, revision schedules for Year 11 were amended to address the area of most need, sixth form mentoring was introduced to help raise achievement at GCSE, the list goes on.

Reflection moment

- When did you last ask your team for feedback?

- How do you try and share ownership?

- Have you ever changed your mind about something after discussing it with the team?

- Do you think your team members would say that you include them and consult with them?

Chapter 7

Using a SWOT Analysis: Identifying Issues and Leading Improvements!

Even if you are a more experienced leader it is good practice to get staff actively involved in reflecting on what is working well and what could be better – rather than just dictatorially announcing what will be the next new initiative! I know some SMTs would have had much more 'buy in' from me if they had done this first! A good tool for managing this in a focused way in a meeting is the use of a SWOT analysis. If you are a Business Studies teacher you will already be adept at using these in your curriculum area, and you will be using them in a much more sophisticated way than indicated below; however, for those of us who aren't business gurus, here is my take on how it can be used to successfully identify issues and plan for improvements within your team or organisation.

The idea is you display a large version of the chart (usually on a flipchart) and use it to start an organised discussion within the team on a specific area. It can be used to guide the discussion, letting staff unpick important issues or areas of concern that need tackling in your area or school. Ideally you should give staff advance warning of the topic to be discussed (always good practice) because then they are more likely to bring along some good ideas to the meeting, but it can just be done on the fly.

Strengths	Weaknesses
Opportunities	Threats

SWOT diagram

1. Firstly, you need to explain to your staff *why* the issue is important. For example, you might want to think about strategies for raising achievement in Year 11, developing extra-curricular provision or tackling an area that a school review or Ofsted inspection has highlighted as an issue, such as raising boys' achievement, improving attendance issues or developing better strategies for tackling bullying. If staff understand *why* the issue is key, then they are more likely to give the task their serious consideration.

2. The first quarter of the diagram allows staff to reflect on the *strengths* in that area. It allows you to reflect on what is already working well and what might be the pockets of good practice within your area. Give out

various different coloured sticky notes and ask staff to use them to note down ideas or aspects that they feel are a current strength. They then place them on the board. It gets the meeting off to a good start because it begins with the positives. It also indicates to staff that you are aware that they already have some good practice going on. You are not seeing yourself as their 'saviour', coming to fix all of their issues, and you are not presuming that they are incompetent or without any ideas and thoughts of their own.

Using a SWOT diagram usually generates some really good ideas. Don't despair if your staff don't come up with any, because even if there aren't any suggestions of positives (and I have never heard of this happening) this can also be used to your advantage – since this highlights that something really needs to be done to address the issue. It leaves the way clear for you to give them some suggestions for new strategies to try out that are working elsewhere. An example of this is seen below:

SWOT in action: Literacy Across the Curriculum

One newly appointed, Whole School Literacy Across the Curriculum coordinator, wanted to raise the profile of this important area in his school. He knew that the provision of this was patchy; a whole school review had identified some strengths and some subjects were doing things very well. However, others weren't and some had yet to 'buy in' to the idea that developing literacy was their concern.

He used the SWOT analysis in a whole staff INSET day to promote the idea of Literacy Across the Curriculum (LAC).

Strengths

This allowed staff from different areas to highlight their strengths or indicate successful activities they were employing in improving LAC in lessons. These included many practical suggestions, such as using word walls (to display key vocabulary), teaching spelling strategies, using a lot of talk for learning in lessons, having an established repertoire of different techniques to teach new vocabulary, etc. Hearing some of these ideas discussed in the meeting, and allowing the staff who had identified the good practice to elaborate a little bit about what it involved, meant that staff who weren't using these strategies heard about them. It also highlighted a bank of good practice (some of it previously unknown) that could be referred to later.

Weaknesses

This relates to barriers, issues and areas of difficulty. For example, with the issue of embedding Literacy Across the Curriculum staff might discuss the following: pupils not having work corrected for literacy errors, pupils not enjoying reading, a lack of staff expertise in teaching literacy skills. The idea of this quadrant also allows the leader to mention some of the weaknesses that they are aware of, perhaps relating to the internal review or latest Ofsted report.

In developing improvements in schools it is important to consider what the real and perceived weaknesses are. One of the issues in leading improvements is that they are often championed by people who really understand the issue and who have mastered the practice, whether that is employing AfL, using ICT effectively, or embedding Literacy Across the Curriculum. Clearly it makes good sense to have an expert leading in the area, but the problem can be that they are such an expert that they forget what it would be like *not* to know a great deal about the issue and not to have ready strategies at their fingertips. Not addressing the real weaknesses means that some areas aren't really tackled; they are glossed over with the assumption that everybody knows what good Literacy Across the Curriculum is when often they don't. Avoiding the honest consideration of weaknesses is a mistake. A good leader needs to be brave and be prepared to listen to whatever people's concerns are so that they can be addressed and improvements can be made.

Opportunities

This is the segment where you can really gear up for leading improvements – it asks you to consider what strategies/opportunities/resources might be available that could be used to solve the issue. What opportunities exist both immediately and in the future? In 'business SWOT analyses' this often looks towards external solutions; however, in schools it is good practice to look internally first, to see what good practice already exists, since there are obvious cost implications with external help. It is also true that schools often need to develop better consistency between different departments and teachers within the school.

Looking at the previous example of Literacy Across the Curriculum, there is a range of different internal opportunities that might be appropriate. One might be for the staff who identify that they already have some good LAC practice happening in lessons to write up a simple strategy (what it is/what they do/why it works). These could be compiled into a directory of LAC ideas, thereby sharing ideas across the school. Maybe those in areas with a particular specialism related to literacy – MFL departments who are often very adept at teaching vocabulary, History departments who teach a lot of discursive arguments and RE departments who do a lot of 'talk for learning' – would be willing to lead a micro training session on this to other staff (fifteen-minute training sessions on these areas later in the term).

Maybe staff will suggest some other opportunities, such as looking at specific resources they know are useful to promote cross-curricular literacy, or maybe you will need to help them generate some. Perhaps the weaknesses will have given staff some ideas to generate solutions of their own; they may have identified that they all need some whole staff training – which could be a topic for your next INSET day. Some might identify improvements that could be made to the school's homework diary so that pupils can record key literacy targets and literacy corrections. Perhaps they think that there are other opportunities that could be developed in tutor time. The list goes on.

This is a dynamic segment for generating a whole range of exciting possibilities. Don't try to clamp down on staff too much here; ideally you want to generate lots of ideas and not have people pulling them apart, saying, 'We tried that at my last school and it didn't work.' This isn't helpful at this stage. The refinement of these ideas and opportunities, and the need to sift through them to find the ones that have potential, is a much later task.

Threats

Finally, we need to look at the possible threats to improvements. This section is not, as one bullish middle leader asked recently on some training, 'Is it where we threaten the team if they don't do what we say?' (Can you imagine if they were *your* team leader?) Instead, it is about the things that can threaten the planned area of improvement. What could derail the project are internal or external threats. For example, the government could make changes to the school curriculum which might take priority over your planned changes (external threat) or additional, external funding for a particular project might cease (another external threat). Subject staff might leave, which is an internal threat. A good leader always considers what are the issues and things that could cause the issue to unravel.

From threats to success!

The following example highlights how a school leadership team looked at potential threats and tried to resolve them. The school was thinking of equipping *all* their students with the latest state-of-the-art technology (in this case iPads), expecting that all pupils' parents would contribute to the funding of the project. It wasn't a very affluent area so the need for funding was a real threat to the success of the project. Making change linked to technology is often fraught with issues about how it is implemented and how staff are trained. Additionally, equipping everybody with the same technology at the same time can produce issues in terms of its shelf life and create real training needs for staff. There is the likelihood with any technology that it will become outdated and need renewing – the average update to a model of equipment is about twelve months.

So, depending on the planned area of improvement, there are different threats. It is important to examine these barriers so that you are able to produce a realistic and achievable plan. For example, with the technology scenario, it would be wise for the school to visit another school who has undertaken this to see the benefits and issues. Or perhaps they could pilot the technology with a smaller group of teachers and plan to roll it out each year, therefore building on successes and removing glitches when the project is limited to a smaller number of teachers. The school would also need to ensure that it had the additional funding available to purchase the necessary hardware if parental generosity wasn't as forthcoming as expected. Other threats could include the fact that the school is involved with a great many other initiatives and may not have the necessary training or capacity to manage all of these successfully.

This segment can also be used to discuss what the threats might be if the planned action to address the issue is not taken at all. With our technology issue above, if the school does not move with the times, introducing and making the best use of ICT to help pupils learn more effectively, then there is a real danger that pupils will become disengaged and that the teachers will lose a valuable opportunity to make learning more engaging, relevant and effective for their students.

Regarding our earlier example of the planned introduction of literacy across the curriculum, if this is not adopted effectively in the school then the school will be found wanting by Ofsted when it is inspected – ensuring that all pupils have good literacy skills and that these are reinforced across the school is an important part of the current Ofsted inspection criteria. Unless key literacy issues are tackled, the school won't equip all of its pupils with the literacy skills needed for everyday life or to enable them to pass examinations successfully.

Chapter 8

Using Previous Inspection Reports

What is happening in lessons right now is much more important than what happened two years ago. We are most interested in the current achievement of pupils – how well are they doing? However, good leaders will make sure that any previous problems have been resolved. I have often run training on preparation for Ofsted and I always ask, 'Do you know what your issues for improvement were in your previous inspection?' And then, 'How successfully have they been resolved?' I am shocked by how many senior managers do not readily have these issues at their fingertips. All Ofsted reports give summary points for development, starting with the most important issues that need improvement. For example, a recent secondary school judged 'good' had the following points to address: 'checking that all students respond to the very helpful marking provided by most teachers' and 'making sure that all teachers fully challenge the most able students'. It would be important as a middle leader to make sure that these issues had been addressed with your department and that any changes were monitored to ensure that things had actually improved.

Even schools that are judged 'outstanding' will usually have at least one recommendation. Your school/area might also have been reviewed by the Local Authority, or an external consultant, and any areas identified here for improvement should also be addressed.

Have previous issues been addressed effectively?

Before an inspection, inspectors will read the previous report and quickly identify whether these issues have been resolved. If they are still an issue and are leading to underachievement of the pupils then it is an indication that the leadership is not good. Most often, the issues highlighted will focus on areas that are applicable across the school, such as 'challenge', but sometimes groups of students are highlighted, such as 'lower ability boys' or even particular subjects are specified as requiring improvement. A really effective middle leader knows what the issues mentioned were and can show that they have been fully addressed (if relevant to their area) and that positive action has taken place.

It is quite possible that during your monitoring you find that these issues are still a concern, and then it is really important to raise them again and make resolving them a priority. If you have already been trying strategies to lead improvements and these don't appear to be working, then it is important to raise this with your SMT link. Explain what the issue is and ask them for advice. It could be that there is an area of the school that is succeeding with this issue and it could assist you. The SMT member might suggest some interventions or they might even give you some time with a consultant who is an expert in that area to help you. It could be that while you have started to tackle this area, the strategies are not yet resolving the issue or the changes are not being thoroughly embedded (see Chapter 30 for more information on how to successfully manage change).

Asking for assistance isn't a weakness, but avoiding the issue is. It is most likely that any issues identified by Ofsted or ISI (Independent Schools Inspectorate) which fall under your area of responsibility will relate to the quality of teaching and learning or management. This could be about providing sufficient challenge in lessons or ensuring feed-back is effective. Here the amazing middle leader might want to make this a focus of lesson observations, an area for departmental training or a focus for team meetings where improvements are discussed, trialled and evaluated. Bear in mind if you are a new middle leader that some of these issues may have existed for a while, and you might not be able to resolve them without assistance from the SMT or some external support.

Thinking point

- Do you think that you are more of a leader than a manager?

- Can you articulate your vision for your department or team?

- When did you last ask your team for feedback on what is going well or what could be even better?

- When might you use a SWOT analysis in discussion with your team?

- Are you aware of the Strengths, Weaknesses, Opportunities and Threats relating to something you are trying to achieve?

- Do you know what the previous issues were in any school or department review? Have you taken steps to address these? How effective has this been?

Chapter 9

Pupil Talk: What Pupils Say!

Great middle leaders are keen to hear from pupils. They seek out pupils' views. They consult pupils regularly to find out what is working, how they are finding the subject, what they are enjoying and what could be better. Pupils are truthful. Pupils tell it as it is. Given that the main purpose of a middle leader is to improve pupils' achievement, progress and enjoyment in their area of the school, it makes sense to ask them how they are feeling and how they find lessons/tutor time/revision programmes/extra-curricular events. What do they find effective, and, of course, what could be better?

Pupils are a very good touchstone for the success or otherwise of an initiative. Imagine that you have decided to look at making pupils more independent and at making teaching more interactive – you correctly identified this as an issue and you've received some 'buy in from staff' (perhaps you even used a SWOT analysis to generate this). You've put into place lots of interventions to deal with the issue: staff have attended training, maybe there's been coaching, an external consultant, new teaching schemes or new resources. However, because you are a great leader you have realised that you can't just tick this off as a job well done. You know that you need to evaluate the success of this initiative. You want to find out whether it has made any difference. Of course, you will have watched some lessons and all staff have been diligent in teaching much more independent lessons. Interviewing pupils is one way of really testing this out. While some staff might nod and appear to agree completely with your marking policy/ideas for teaching revision/implementation of the behaviour policy, the reality of whether they are actually doing this and whether it is effective is shown in what the pupils say and do in lessons and the outcomes of their learning.

There are different ways of getting to hear 'pupil voice' and these will be discussed below. Before you start, it is important that you think about what it is you really want to find out from the students and then think about the most appropriate means for doing so.

Interviewing small groups of pupils in a semi-structured interview

Here you get together about eight pupils and ask them questions about the issue you are interested in. You can even get them to bring along examples of their work to illustrate their points. (This also gives you valuable information about the quality of the marking and whether pupils actually understand and act on the teachers' comments!) In an hour's lesson you could see three groups of eight students for about twenty minutes each. This gives you a really good overview of the experiences and attitudes of a year group, particularly if you are sure to select pupils from across the age and ability range. You might ask for pupils from top sets for the first session or they could be grouped in other ways depending on the issue you are addressing; for example, groups of all boys or girls.

Ofsted often favour this approach when interviewing pupils to find out about an issue or to test a hypothesis (perhaps they suspect that pupils aren't really understanding how they can make their work better and they want to see if this is true). It is an effective strategy, and although you will have already planned the questions you want answered, the fact that it is a discussion means you can ask follow-up questions and get pupils to elaborate on a point. This is not possible in a written questionnaire and students are often happier to expand their ideas verbally rather than by writing them down. It also means that if pupils mention something in passing that you did not expect – 'What is it you like best about your Science lessons?' 'I love Science because we never get set any homework' – you have the opportunity to probe this response, to see if it is common within the group and indicates a real issue with homework, or to see whether it is just that the Science teacher has set them a longer term project for a few weeks so the home-work isn't due in just yet.

When interviewing pupils, it is a good idea to explain *why* you are doing it and *what you hope to achieve*. I usually say something like this: 'We are keen to make History lessons the best they can be and we want to ask you some questions about your experiences in History.' Or, 'I don't want to know individual teacher names, but I am going to ask you about your experiences in French lessons/tutor time/after-school clubs. We will use this information to help us with our teaching/lead improvements/review our revision programme.'

Bear in mind that it can often be a good idea to ask another middle leader or a consultant to conduct the interview for you. This is because sometimes we are so close to the issue that we ask leading questions; perhaps we have invested a lot of energy into trying to develop things, so if we hear slightly negative feedback we gloss over it rather than really hearing what it can tell us to improve. Additionally, pupils are very aware of your role in school, and if they like you they might put a much more positive spin on French lessons to you than they would if you had asked a head of department from another area to interview your pupils about your subject.

Questionnaires

Sometimes you will want to survey a much larger group of pupils. You don't want to just delve into the experiences of a sample group – you want to know how *all* of Year 9 found the option experience, or you want to survey *all* of Year 6 about their reading habits. This is where paper questionnaires and online surveys can be really useful. Paper surveys are easier to draw up and administer, they are easy to distribute and they are clear to understand and apply. The difficulties are that some pupils don't want to add longer answers and you have the time-consuming issue of 'crunching the responses'. A good leader should have the vision to put the questionnaire together and be interested in using the results to drive forward improvements – not doing the admin. There is a large administrative demand in counting and summarising the responses, so it is important to check that you have the necessary admin support before you plan to undertake this.

There is a range of online questionnaires, many of which are free. These have the great advantage that they can distil and crunch the data for you, often by just clicking a button. Of course, you may find that you need IT assistance in setting up the questionnaires, but you might discover some already written on the topic you are interested in that that you can easily adapt. Obviously, creating your own questionnaire is the most useful thing you can do because you can ask the questions that you really want to know the answers to. However, it is useful to have a look at some ready-made questionnaires to help you save time.

Schools that have used online surveys comment that it is a good idea to ensure that the pupils have the time and opportunity to complete these in school to ensure a full completion rate and so that questions can be explained. You might need to negotiate some time to do this. The main surveys that are used in schools (although new ones are developing all the while) are Yacapaca and Survey Monkey, a free online survey and questionnaire tool.

Below are some suggested questions that can be used for surveys and questionnaires:

- What do you like about Maths lessons?

- What do you think could be improved in your Maths lessons?

- Do you regularly answer questions in class?

- Do you think you have to work hard in lessons?

- Do you understand what you need to do to achieve in Maths lessons?

- Do you get the opportunity to work in pairs and groups in lessons?

- Do you know what your target level/grade is?

- Do you know what you need to do to achieve it?

- Do you feel that you are making good progress in Maths?

- How does the work you are doing this year in Maths compare to last year?

- When your book is marked do you understand what you need to do to improve your work?

Other advantages with online surveys are that pupils can be surveyed about an area *before* you put strategies for improvement into place and *afterwards*. This gives you some hard evidence to show the improvements that have been made or to give you feedback about why things still need work. This is a really important consideration because interviewing pupils isn't an end in itself, rather it is one method of receiving information about what the current state of play is. It allows you to consider what is working and what could be improved.

Use the results to improve practice!

The results of a survey can also be used to galvanise staff and get them to see that the proposed change is really needed. In one school, when I was about to lead some training on Assessment for Learning, the head of department displayed the results of a questionnaire that she had used with staff and then used with whole year groups of pupils. It included pertinent questions relating to AfL, such as: Do you feel that you get helpful feedback on your work? Do you regularly get the opportunity to answer questions in class? Do you know what your target grade is? She highlighted what staff's surveys showed: they believed that the feedback they gave to students was a fantastic 95%, but they felt that a much smaller percentage of pupils would feel that they were involved and could answer questions in class (just under 70%).

In fact, the pupils returned a very different response – they did feel very involved in lessons and felt that they answered a great deal (over 90% of pupils felt that they regularly answered questions). However, they did not feel that they received helpful feedback or that their books were marked regularly; less than 50% felt this! Given that the topic of my training was on 'ensuring good feedback to pupils' this meant that staff had a real 'buy in', not only to listen to what I said, but to take action on it. The middle leader also discussed how they were going to follow up on this area: using book scrutinies to see whether this really was an issue, and ensuring that pupils knew what the marking meant so that they could do something useful with the corrections.

Thinking point

Seeking pupils' opinions on our practice is expected by Ofsted and if it is done correctly it is invaluable in identifying what is working well and will help guide you in making things even better! Think about what you might want to ask your students and how this could be useful to you as a leader and your team as a whole. Will you get your team involved in selecting the questions?

Reflection moment

- What questions would you really like to ask students?

- Which group or type of students do you think you should start with? What makes you select these students?

- How will you schedule it within the year? Ideally you will want to take action and then make time to re-question the students at a later date. This will help you to evaluate the impact of your actions.

- Who might you need to ask support from to help with the practicalities of arranging the questionnaires? This might involve arranging some technical or administrative support or making time for pupils to take the questionnaire.

- Who is already doing this in school? How can you ensure that you are not duplicating efforts?

Three things I think I would like to investigate in my area of responsibility are:

1.

2.

3.

Chapter 10

Knowing Where We Are: Using Data!

Looking carefully at the data can give you an indication of where there is very good practice and where things might need improving. Clearly there is a lot of data, both internally produced by the school and externally, that will inform you about the current state of your area.

A good middle leader is very aware of what the current data is telling them. Data should come from your SMT link and your job should be looking for trends and patterns, picking out individuals that are underachieving, tracking their progress and enacting improvements. A middle leader should not be inputting data themselves and spending hours doing so – that is the job of a competent admin assistant. If you find that you are being asked to do lots of administrative tasks linked to data, hold this page in front of your SMT or refer them to the workforce agreement! Your job as a leader is to spot trends and track pupil progress, making plans to effectively tackle underachievement. It is to act to raise achievement with students; it is not to be hunched over a laptop typing in lots of numbers – that is not leadership.

There are a range of things you need to know about data.

Some of these are straightforward and some will require more detailed enquiry:

- What is the current state of play – what are pupils achieving right now?

- If your subject has coursework or controlled assessments, how are these progressing? Are pupils up to date and on track to achieve their targets? How does this relate to their prospective examination results or other tests?

- What are their targets? Depending on your school type, the targets will be different and the ways of generating them may be different – state schools will have different information to independent schools. Core curriculum subjects – English, Maths and Science – will also have more specific detail than non-core subjects.

- How far is the gap between pupils' current work and their targets? You need to have systems to track this. Most schools will have systems where pupils who are working below a target are flagged in a different colour.

- What are the trends over time? Ofsted looks at the trends over the last three years so it is important to know this. How have results been over the last three years? If results have been steadily climbing and meeting or exceeding targets this is likely to indicate aspects of good leadership. If results seem to have been stuck or declining in the last three years then this is clearly an issue. So be aware of your trends and how they are broken down by pupil group. For example, if lower ability GCSE boys underachieved in 2012, but their achievement rose in 2013 and continued well into 2014 then this might suggest continuing improvement with this group.

- What are the figures for participation rates? This really applies to option subjects. If for the last two years the number taking a History GCSE has drastically declined then this is an indication that things might not be as good as they could be. You might also want to survey pupils to find out why they have opted to take your subject or chosen another instead. They might be opting out because of poor teaching or it might be another reason – you need to find out!

- Do all pupils complete the course and do they all receive an award? If there are courses with a number of pupils failing to gain any award then this might indicate issues in achievement or it might indicate pupils are being directed towards taking courses that are not best suited to their needs. There is a huge range of certificated courses, as well as the traditional GCSEs – it is important to ensure that pupils are taking the right ones for them. The weakest students should be on an appropriate course so that they can gain some skill and certification, even if it is not a GCSE.

- How well are individuals and different groups of students achieving? A great leader knows that all of their pupils need to achieve and this is echoed by Ofsted. *All* groups of pupils should achieve their potential. This means knowing what the groups are, looking at how they are doing, monitoring them and putting into place any techniques to raise achievement if groups appear to be underachieving – and knowing how effective any of these measures have been.

- What are you doing to bridge any gaps between the current state and targets? What plans do you have? How are they progressing? How effective are your interventions?

- If you are an examination subject you will also receive specific breakdowns for pupils' performance on different exam papers and, with most examination boards, this can also be accessed at question level too. This means that you can 'drill down into the data' and see which questions pupils are succeeding with and which are posing a challenge. If you are unsure what your examination board offers, then a brief chat to the subject officer of the exam board can inform you of this. Look up their details on their web site.

- Are your staff aware of the pupils' targets? Do they know who might be underachieving and what they need to do to address this?

Pastoral leaders and data

The data you need will differ depending on your area of expertise; if you are a pastoral leader you will, of course, be interested in the headline figures for pupil achievement. Unlike a subject leader who will be drilling down to the particular grades and specific detail of their subject you will be looking at things more widely. How many students are achieving five A*–C grades including English and Maths? How is the school meeting any other external government measures of achievement? Are they selecting the right type of qualification for their pupils' individual needs?

You will also be very aware of individual students and their specific needs. You will want to know and evaluate what sorts of interventions are offered across the school to make sure that pupils do the best they can. Are any departments dropping the ball? You will be using the data to highlight which pupils are at risk and which are on track, providing suitable guidance to ensure that all pupils achieve their best whether they are a predicted A* or E.

It is also about having detailed knowledge of the pupils' achievements as individuals and in groups across the board.

You will need to know what is being done to secure the achievement of your 'at risk' pupils, as well as understanding groups of students and resolving any particular barriers to achievement – such as above average absence rates which can impact on results. As a pastoral or year group leader you will have a unique insight into how individual pupils are progressing in a range of subjects and you will be using your expertise to share good practice and to tackle any areas that might be underachieving. You are also likely to be involved in helping departments make best use of any additional government funding designed to help vulnerable pupils achieve – such as the Pupil Premium funding.

Reflection moment

- Do you have the data you need to help you evaluate your current position?

- Do you know who to ask in school to provide you with the data?

- What further information would help you?

- What three things does the data tell you are working well?

- What three areas of groups need further attention?

Chapter 11

Actions from the Data – Involving the Team

When I first started as a middle leader I can remember being told that I had a very high (seemingly impossible) target to meet for the A–C pass rate. I can remember leaving the meeting deeply troubled about how *I* would achieve it, as if it was just *my* issue. Obviously the head of department needs to lead the way with their team, ensuring that pupils' progress is monitored, but success only happens when individuals across the whole team take active individual responsibility for achievement and take consistent actions to improve things. It is important that leaders ensure that all staff are aware of their own responsibilities and that they know how to carry them out. These include:

- Knowing the ability range and targets of all the pupils in the class.

- Using this information to make lessons suit-able for all learners, challenging and differentiating where necessary.

- Providing good, regular feedback on work that pupils find helpful.

- Helping individual pupils understand their targets and developing strategies in classes for getting them to reflect on what they can do well and what they need to do next.

- Tracking attendance in the class and liaising with middle leaders regarding any issues.

- Knowing pupils well and being aware of any factors that might cause them to have specific needs and sharing this information. Liaising with other staff or teachers to ensure any additional intervention classes or programmes are put in place and monitoring their effectiveness.

Improvements don't happen, though, unless *all* staff take responsibility for tackling underachievement. This is why a good middle leader needs to have regular conversations with team members to discuss what they are doing with particular pupils and how effective it has been.

Thinking point

- Can your staff answer the questions above? Are there any areas that might need revisiting in department time?

- Do staff use this information actively so that they are planning and delivering lessons that are best suited to their pupils' needs?

- Do you check that staff have all of the necessary information, guidance and training required to help them do their job effectively?

- Do you discuss targets and current grade expectations with staff, both as a department target and per teaching class?

- Do you have simple systems for tracking pupil progress against targets so that you can see which pupils are underperforming? Do you have strategies to address this with the teacher and with any external interventions?

Chapter 12

Strategies for Leading Improvement Relating to Pupils' Achievement

There are key actions that an outstanding head of department will ensure are happening to help maintain high standards and show how they are leading improvements. These might include:

- **Leading the moderation of work**

    Leading this within the team and in some cases across schools, particularly where there are separate infant/junior schools. It is important that everybody is clear what a B grade/level 5 piece of work looks like, otherwise the data you have will be inaccurate. Teams that regularly look at and share work to set a common standard find that expectations and standards are raised because staff are more familiar with what good work looks like, and they are aware of what pupils need to do next to get to the next level. This will become increasingly important as grades, levels and criteria are changed and adapted.

- **Establishing training for areas of development**

    Sometimes not enough pupils gain the higher grades because staff don't actually know what an A* response looks like. Be aware that as a middle leader you may have an enormous amount of subject-specific expertise that other staff might not have. Staff might have been teaching middle ability groups for a number of years and may lack the subject-specific expertise to teach the higher level; or staff may need advice for teaching 'coasting' middle-set pupils or those with specific needs. A good leader knows their staff's strengths and weaknesses and addresses these. A member of staff might have a First in Biology from Oxford but still be inexperienced in knowing and understanding the specific nuances needed for teaching GCSE Biology, because of the very exacting (and often changing) requirements of the examination board's specifications.

- **Showing examples of pupils who have made progress and exploring reasons why some pupils appear 'stuck'**

  Can you discuss an example of a pupil where they appeared stuck at a certain level or where they were underachieving and they were successfully moved on owing to teaching strategies or interventions? It is well worth writing down and sharing these examples within the department so that teachers can learn from each other and see what they need to do to move pupils up a level. It is also a good idea to write an example up and attach evidence as an exemplar of good practice for Ofsted and to show other staff about the steps you have taken to lead improvements.

- **Initiating changes to schemes of work**

  This is done to add rigour or challenge or to increase opportunities for Assessment for Learning strategies. Although it is important to ensure that schemes of work are helpful, it can be too easy to get carried away generating paperwork that can make you feel you are leading improvements, when actually you are just being very busy. Schemes of work are only helpful if they are used and if staff are able to adapt them to meet the needs of the individuals in their classes. Spending days rewriting schemes of work won't raise achievement; noting the weaknesses in the schemes, sharing these with the team and agreeing what teaching strategies will be used to deliver great lessons might.

- **Department planning to raise standards**

  So if, for example, there is underachievement across Year 8 in writing, what whole department strategies are being put into place? This might involve particular schemes of work, strategies or training for those teachers teaching these pupils.

- **Additional external interventions**

  It might be the case that some pupils need extra timetabled help. Obviously it is crucial that the pupils' actual timetabled lessons are really good, because this is where they are the majority of the time. But it could be the case that some pupils need some extra intervention, additional classes, one-to-one tutoring or some pastoral mentoring relating to an area that is causing them issues (this will vary but could include personal organisation, completing homework or building their self-esteem). It might be that there is a group of pupils who need additional coaching to develop weak literacy or numeracy skills.

One school, for example, had twenty girls in Year 11 who had the potential to do well, but faced a crippling lack of self-confidence which really stymied their approach in lessons and exams. Under the leadership of the head of

Year 11, this school planned a whole programme incorporating study skills with raising confidence and team building, boosting the students' belief that they could achieve. This is where middle leaders need to be strategic. They have analysed the data and now they need to appropriate more plans for intervention and assess how effective they have been.

Chapter 13

Discovering Exceptional Practice and Forging Useful Networks

It is important to know where examples of outstanding practice are so that you can benchmark your own practice against them and, most importantly, adopt and adapt any useful strategies. In order to do this it is important to know what exceptional practice is and to compare your area against this. Sometimes this can be quite difficult, particularly if you have only been in one school, so where can you find other good practice?

Who does it better? Visiting other schools

One of the best CPD experiences I had as a middle leader was when I visited another school. I had been working at my school for a year, I had put into place the obvious improvements that I could see needed doing, I had looked at the school's previous Ofsted report and Local Authority reviews, and I had noted what improvements needed to be made from my lesson observations and discussions with pupils. However, I didn't always know what the 'best' schools were doing and although I was clear on some of the areas that needed improvement, I wasn't always clear on the best way of achieving this. I wanted to see some really exceptional practice.

I asked a local adviser if she could give me an example of a school that had a similar intake of pupils to mine, but was achieving much more with them and had a head of department who would be approachable. I got one lesson covered in the afternoon (I was free for the rest of the day) and at lunchtime I left to visit a school twenty miles away. I had a list of questions and met a really helpful, slightly more experienced head of department and I basically ransacked her brain. What was she doing for x? What resources did she find most useful? You get the picture. After just a couple of hours, I had loads of ideas, but most importantly she had explained to me the perils and pitfalls behind implementing them. I don't think she got a great deal out of the meeting – aside from experiencing that great glow of expertise that envelops you when somebody notes down your every word – but for me it was a massively useful exercise. Visiting somebody who was away from my school environment meant that I could ask those questions that I really felt I should have known the answers to, but didn't. She was a subject expert, running the same exam specification with similar pupils, so all of the suggestions were really relevant and useful, much more so than asking for general strategies from another subject leader in my own school.

I would really encourage you to visit another local school, but one with a similar type of pupil in a similar area, and one that is just a bit more successful. Of course, there are things you can learn from any school but you will find the practice easier to replicate if the students are taking similar courses and have similar backgrounds.

For obvious reasons it can be difficult to arrange visits out of school and the success of a visit depends not just on picking the right school, but meeting a subject leader who is happy to share ideas. However, it is legitimate CPD and can be much more effective and much less costly than a day's INSET training.

Ofsted surveys of good practice

One easy way of gaining a wider slice of good practice, and one that can very easily be achieved from the comfort of home/school, is to use the Ofsted website. I never used to look at the website before I became an adviser (unless I was planning to move schools and I wanted to find out what the prospective school was really like). However, I had missed a trick.

Ofsted undertake good practice surveys and produce a range of free online publications. They visit a wide range of schools (both primary and secondary) and colleges to investigate current practice. They write reports showcasing good practice and highlighting the key issues in the area/subject. If you are a subject coordinator, in, say, mathematics, you will be delighted to learn that there is a maths publication detailing the current issues in teaching and learning, curriculum, management and standards. These are currently completed on a regular basis for different subjects and for different aspects that are pertinent to schools. You might be leading on a specific area, such as Gifted and Talented (G&T) achievement, boys' achievement or ICT, and there are useful publications or case studies on many areas.

In order to find these surveys and publications, first go to the Ofsted website: www.ofsted.gov.uk and search in publications or surveys or advanced research. If somebody waves a useful looking survey at you on training ask them what the specific reference number is or publication date as this will make it easier to find.

These reports and surveys are particularly useful because they detail not only what the current issues are, but they include examples of good practice from a variety of state schools. They also give a clear overview about practice across the country and provide useful information about primary and secondary schools which is very useful for transition information. I have found one of the most useful ways to use them is to take three different coloured high-lighter pens and use them as I look at the issues: green (I feel that my area is already doing this well), amber (we do bits of this but maybe there are some ideas here to con-sider further), red (we don't do this; possibly we should). You can quickly skim through the report and use this to help you decide on any areas that you need to develop. For example, on one occasion I was helping a Maths team look at improving the marking and feedback they were giving to students – using the most recent Maths report allowed me to show annotated examples of good marking and less effective marking.

Extracts from these reports can be used to highlight good practice to your team. They are effective because they are clearly written and they show examples of good ideas. Using clear examples is one way of showing your team what other successful schools are achieving.

Using other people's expertise and forums

A good middle leader builds a network of colleagues and friends so that they can ask people for advice and have a range of sounding boards. They should also be prepared to offer suggestions in return. When attending CPD events, exam-board meetings or even social occasions, there is bound to be a fellow teacher about with some useful infor-mation at their fingertips. Try to exchange contact details and share ideas about resources/strategies with other teachers and middle leaders you meet who are on the same wavelength and who are tackling similar issues. Finding out how other people have dealt with things is extremely useful and is a great time saving method, as well as a good way of unearthing some real gems.

I am a great fan of having at least *five fabulous connections* in the area that you are working in. Here's an example of how it can work. Recently I was asked to help a school out in developing a particular area which was brand new. Before I started thinking, I sent out an email to five friends/colleagues asking if any of them had done anything similar and whether they would be willing to share their ideas. I received messages back: one giving me a whole scheme of work, one sending a useful 'work in progress', another directing me to some useful online resources that I had been unaware of and two replying that they hadn't done it yet, so could I send them *my* work after I had completed it! When exchanging useful information and making the most of these networks it is important to make sure that you are a giver, not always a taker – I know my heart sinks when I get emails from a couple of people who are always just asking for 'one more thing' but who are always too busy to respond to my occasional requests.

Forums and Subject Associations

If you don't have a good network then remember that online forums can be an incredibly useful way of developing a helpful network of support. TES has a useful forum (www.tes.co.uk) with every area listed, from subject-specific areas to personal issues – it's the only place where you can find both tips to raise attendance and fabulous recipes for cooking with leftovers! While you might not wish to post a question yourself, scanning through the postings from others from time to time will alert you to the other main issues that other middle leaders are considering. It is a quick way to find out if you are on track or if there is an issue or future concern that you should be aware of.

One head of Drama following a thread about the new exam specification realised that she had misunderstood an aspect of the new course design. For her, reading other posters' comments and a reference to the exam specification meant she avoided a mistake that could have cost her students a great deal.

Exam boards often have forums and post updates on Twitter, and you can sign up for email updates. This is well worth doing as they often reference useful resources, give training titbits and sometimes even send examples of schemes of work, all of which save time and keep you skilled up. Contacting the subject officer in person by phone can often be very fruitful. Some exam boards are particularly helpful on the phone and you can speak straight to the person who knows the answer. One head of department told me she had telephoned one subject officer in despair after her school received some, in her words, 'awful results' in the first year after changing the exam board. The subject officer was so sympathetic to her plight that she actually arranged a free twilight training session for her department at the school! (I wouldn't suggest that this is common practice at all, but it is true that when exam boards are vying for new schools they can be very accommodating and a smart middle leader seeks to make the most of it.)

Twitter – peek into other people's classrooms

Twitter is an incredibly useful way of connecting and interacting with other middle leaders and subject specialists online. Twitter is easy to get started with and basically allows you to send and receive short messages or 'tweets' of up to 140 characters. As a middle leader it gives you a fantastic opportunity to hear what other middle leaders are doing and, if you wish, to interact with them. I have discovered many incredibly useful links, including lesson resources, quick answers to questions and queries about strategies and ideas to try out.

Unlike Facebook, you can easily 'unfollow' anybody without causing offence, and there's no need to post anything yourself unless you wish to. It is quite permissible to lurk and mine other people's good ideas without posting anything yourself.

There is a wide range of useful educationalists to follow (not forgetting the odd celebrity to liven up your Twitter feeds). Many of them write interesting blogs or link their tweets to handy online resources.

My top ten to follow (in no particular order):

@RealGeoffBarton – for Literacy Across the Curriculum, leadership and English

@joedale – for useful ICT developments and MFL ideas

@mrprcollins – for Maths ideas and generally useful teaching strategies

@Teachers Toolkit – for useful teaching, learning and leadership advice

@LA_McDermott – fabulous tips for humanities, particularly History

@Jobaker9 – Art and Design, creative ideas on teaching and learning

@kevbartle – plenty of good ideas and good sense!

@Jivespin – interesting teaching ideas, book recommendations and History tips

@icpjones – head of languages, many useful insights on teaching, learning and ICT

@ASTsupportAAli – range of interesting teaching and learning ideas

And of course, do feel that you can follow me @RealCBD!

Take care with Twitter though and think carefully about what you post. Most teachers use it very professionally but some do post inappropriate comments about their school, staff or even pupils! As a rule of thumb, I don't post anything that I would be unhappy about if it was picked up and quoted in a national newspaper – keep it professional and let your staff be amazed at all the innovative and time saving ideas that you glean from it!

Subject Associations

Don't forget about subject associations – these produce really good resources, hold training events and distil essential information that is pertinent to school subject leaders. They often have forums and many free resources and publications. Subscriptions can be pricey, but this is something that you can legitimately pay for with your department's budget rather than from your own pocket. Please see pages 265–268 for a list of subject associations.

Thinking point

It is important to remember that being a great leader isn't about working the hardest, it is about being the most effective! Using examples and ideas from other people and organisations is not only time-smart, but it also allows you to profit from their good ideas and be aware of the pitfalls in any new practice you are planning.

Reflection moment

- How many 'useful connections' do you have? Where might you have opportunities to develop more of these?

- What do you currently do to peek inside other middle leader's departments? What other opportunities might there be?

- Do you share resources and ideas that you have, both within school and beyond, so that you have a 'bank of goodwill' to draw on?

- Do you make good use of any advisers or subject associations you have? Do you regularly check their websites to ensure that you are up to date?

Three things I want to do to forge useful networks (Idea, Date, Impact):

1.

2.

3.

Section III

Monitoring, Marking and Making Improvements

Chapter 14

Why is Monitoring Important?

Monitoring is an important part of a middle leader's role. Effective monitoring means that you know what the current state of play is within your area of responsibility, whether it's teaching and learning, behaviour, assessment or running a particular subject or course. Good monitoring means you know what is working well and what needs improving. Effective monitoring is, however, more than just taking the temperature of things. Effective monitoring means that when you introduce changes or develop improvements you can check how effectively these initiatives have been embedded. It means that you can amend things accordingly, making sure that improvements continue to grow and flourish.

Monitoring teaching and learning

One of the most important areas of responsibility for all middle leaders is achieving and maintaining high standards in the area of teaching and learning. It is essential that middle leaders strive for the best teaching and learning possible, driving forward improvements across their departments. In years past, a deputy head or senior teacher would know the quality of teaching across the school and be able to identify good practice, taking steps to improve less effective practice.

Today middle leaders are seen as crucial in both auditing and leading improvements in their departments. Developing outstanding teaching and learning should not just be the responsibility of the SMT – if nothing else, with some secondary schools having over ninety staff it is impractical if this is undertaken by the SMT alone. Moreover, it is the middle leaders who have the subject-specific knowledge, coupled with an understanding of effective teaching methodologies, who can ensure that improvements really happen in teaching and learning in the classroom.

Chapter 15

Conducting Lesson Observations

Middle leaders need to be skilled at sampling lessons, judging the quality of teaching and learning, and knowing what to do next to embed good practice and make things even better. Inspectors might ask middle leaders to be involved in joint lesson observations during inspections because they will be judging how far middle leaders can accurately judge teaching and learning, whether they give useful feedback to staff and how accurately this relates to the school's own judgements about the quality of teaching and learning.

Most schools will have a cycle of lesson observations and you are advised to work within this. Of course, you may rightly want to complete some of your own additional observations, or start some learning walks (whereby you dip into a number of lessons for short periods of time, looking at a specific issue, such as independent learning, AFL or questioning). These can all be valuable. I would, however, advise that you share your plans with your SMT link to ensure that you haven't arranged lesson observations the same week that the SMT decide to complete reviews of your area. If your team feels pressured or overwhelmed by observations then they might understandably feel hostile. We have to remember that constant observation without a clear purpose doesn't improve things, it just reaffirms what their state is and can actually alienate staff. There's nothing like the stress of constant scrutiny!

What happens when staff don't want to be observed?

Observing lessons gives you a sound starting place for evaluating your team and it should help you decide on any steps for improvement. You need to know the quality of teaching of *all* your team members. Quite often, when I am doing a school review, I will ask a head of department to tell me about the quality of teaching of their staff members. So Ofsted might well ask you, 'Where will I see some particularly effective GCSE teaching?' or, 'Where will I see a really good Phonics session?' You do need to know who is frequently outstanding or consistently good. Of course, people are sometimes inconsistent; we are all human after all! But it is important to know how your staff members usually teach.

Remember though, that even if you plan for your lesson observations to be supportive, staff can still feel threatened by them. As good leaders we need to look at some techniques we can use to minimise this. As a new department leader, I was initially surprised when my team weren't keen for me to observe them; their reluctance was palpable and they kept designing tests and assessments when I suggested a date to watch their lesson. Eventually I suggested that they should come to watch me for a lesson first of all (as individual observers rather than a posse!). They jumped at the chance and I received some useful feedback about my practice. Of course, it was then much more difficult for them to try and wriggle out of a return visit. It would have been very easy for me to have pulled rank and insisted that I was coming in; after all, having lessons observed is an important part of performance management, but I always try the 'carrot approach' first. Most of us much prefer to be encouraged, rather than coerced, into action.

Walk the talk!

My staff were intrigued at the idea of seeing me teach and I also think that this was a useful leadership mantra: never ask anybody to do something that you would not be willing to do yourself! Of course, had my carrot approach not proved effective, then I would have had the 'stick' in reserve (you *have* to have your lessons observed for performance management), and finally, the very big stick – appealing to the SMT to help me reinforce this. As it was, this was unnecessary and I gained much more goodwill from my team by my approach.

Having a line manager in your lesson can feel threatening. Once, when doing a supportive pre-Ofsted visit in a local school, all of the teachers in the team were incredibly nervous, despite my protestations that as their adviser, I was there to help them get ready for inspection. Lesson plans were given to me with trembling hands, although most of the lessons I observed were very good, and those that were not good were only limited in their quality by the nervousness of the teacher (which meant that they rushed their instructions or quashed their probing questions).

When I asked them why they were so nervous, some explained that they did not know what made a great lesson. They were unsure what I was looking for and expecting to see; the criteria for good lessons had never been explained to them. They also added that their subject leader had created great anxiety by commenting that morning in the department office, 'We are being reviewed – we're all doomed!' Creating panic and passing on your anxiety to others certainly isn't the skill of a great leader – some SMTs need to learn this! It is important, however, to unpick what makes a great lesson with your team, so that they know what to expect and have confidence in how they are teaching.

Chapter 16

What Makes Lessons Outstanding?

All teams are different and they will have individuals within them with varying degrees of skill, experience and confidence. It is important to develop strategies to help staff understand what is expected of them and how they can improve performance. Doing this also reduces stress and anxiety because they help illuminate what is necessary for a really effective lesson. You might want to share some of these strategies with staff, dip into them where appropriate, or you might have some better ideas of your own. However you decide to improve your staff's know-how is up to you, but it is really important that all teachers (and teaching assistants) are clear about what makes a great lesson and that they are helped to develop effective strategies for managing this themselves.

So what makes an outstanding lesson?

There are several important areas to consider when looking at teaching outstanding lessons. The questions below are useful to help your team consider what they need to be doing to achieve success. They can be easily adapted as a departmental checklist to assist staff in planning their lessons. At the very least they need sharing and discussing with your team. These are the areas that Ofsted or other observers will consider when judging the quality of teaching and learning in lessons.

The key questions: How much progress are the pupils making? What have they gained as a result of being in the lesson? How are they also progressing across time – from lesson to lesson and over a longer period of time?

- **How are *all* pupils' progressing?**

  Check that there aren't groups of pupils already finished or struggling with the work. The lesson should be meeting *all* pupils' needs and challenging them appropriately. For it to be outstanding, pupils need to be making 'rapid and sustained progress'.[1]

- **Do staff know who all their pupils are and any important information about their learning needs?**

  Is this information about pupils used so that all pupils are challenged? If you are a primary teacher with the same class every day this will obviously be much easier than for a secondary Music teacher who will potentially be teaching hundreds of different pupils. Some schools have designed colour coded seating plans so that staff can give observers a plan of where different pupils are sitting; for example, pupils who are the most able, those who have English as an additional language (EAL), those who have special educational needs (SEN), those for whom the pupil premium provides support and any other groups particular to your setting. This is also a useful reminder to the class teacher about their pupils' needs and helps them to think about whether they are addressing these needs effectively.

---

[1] Ofsted, Evaluation Schedule in the *School Inspection Handbook*, 2014, Ref. 120101.

- **Does the teacher have good subject knowledge?**

  Is there a range of engaging and appropriate teaching strategies being employed? Do these have a good effect on the quality of learning in the lesson? Do they ensure that pupils are actively engaged in their learning?

- **Do pupils receive effective verbal and written feedback?**

  Do they know what they need to do to improve their work and are they supported in doing so? Do they respond to corrections and does their work show good progress over time?

- **If teaching assistants are in the lesson, how are they adding value?**

  Do they help pupils make great progress, ensuring that they are supporting the pupils in gaining better independence and not doing the work for them? Remember, if teaching assistants are working one-to-one with a pupil they are actually teaching them and will be judged accordingly by Ofsted!

- **Questioning: is it appropriate?**

  Does it involve all pupils and does it push pupils to further their knowledge and develop their skills? Many teachers fail to push students enough, accepting their first answer instead of challenging them. It is also important that *all* pupils have an opportunity to respond to questions and even ask them. Watch out for teachers that answer their own questions and dominate discussions! Do teaching assistants pose effective questions to the pupils they are working with rather than telling them the answers?

- **Resources: are they useful, appropriate and do they aid learning?**

  This includes the appropriate use of ICT. Always consider if there are enough resources for pupils and their suitability.

- **Are literacy and numeracy skills reinforced across the curriculum?**

  This might include highlighting key vocabulary, sharing strategies for learning key words, giving strategies for improving reading skills and reinforcing how to draw an appropriate graph or interpret data correctly.

- **Is time used effectively?**

  Does the lesson move on in a purposeful way? Time is not wasted by delays in dealing with equipment or dealing with repeated behavioural issues.

- **Homework: is it set in a timely fashion? (Not just in a rush right at the end!)**

  Is the homework set appropriate and challenging? Does it reinforce learning effectively? Is homework assessed and valued by the teacher?

Thinking point

It is worth asking your team which areas they think are most challenging and even adopting one of these areas as a focus for lesson observations, such as looking at the idea of questioning within a lesson.

The focus of what makes an outstanding lesson has changed in recent years and some teachers may still be coming to terms with this. Their previous experience might have been that an occasional exciting lesson (modelled on the Robbie Williams school of teaching – 'Let Me Entertain You!' – whereby the teacher expends enormous effort in trying to entertain and excite their charges) was sufficient but this no longer works. This is because observers are rightly looking at the impact of the lesson on the pupils and are looking to see that pupils are engaged and learning – not just being the passive recipients of knowledge.

Reflection moment

Which of these areas do you think are the most important areas for your department? Have you shared with them the latest Ofsted criteria for making judgements about the quality of teaching and learning in lessons? Select one thing that you think you need to do as a priority and a couple that you need to investigate over the next term.

---

1. Top priority:

2. Things I need to share or develop with my team over the next term.

3.

Chapter 17

Five Things to Do to Improve Teaching and Learning

Five tips I have found effective when working with teams in raising the standard of lessons are listed below:

1. **Develop a shared understanding of what makes an outstanding lesson!**

    Ask your team what they think makes an outstanding lesson and get them to jot it down on a sticky note. Get them to think about their recent lessons and to discuss when they think they have been successful in a specific area. For example, if somebody mentions 'questioning', ask them what they think makes outstanding questioning and when they think they have achieved this.

    Give out the Ofsted criteria on outstanding teaching and learning – the most recent version can be found at www.ofsted.gov.uk under teaching and learning on the Evaluation Schedule (please note that Ofsted doesn't currently have criteria for single lessons; its criteria are for teaching and learning across the school). It can be adapted as often as three times a year, so it is worth looking at the current version.

    Get staff to use coloured highlighter pens to identify the areas they think they are most effective at and those in which they think they could use more guidance. Use these to action plan some training/ INSET/meeting headlines for your team for the coming term. If you need guidance in tackling each area, consider the book list at the back of this guide. It gives recommendations for easy to access resources on improving teaching and learning. Many of these have interactive activities that can be used to provide checklists or mini department INSETs on these areas.

One teacher I met on a training course before the summer holiday told me everyone in her department had been given a different teaching book for summer holiday reading, linked to the area of outstanding lessons; they had to feedback five useful ideas at the start of the Autumn term. This is a simple way of helping staff update their knowledge. You could take a leaf out of their book and even ask each team member to research areas to develop and feedback on!

2. Show them what outstanding looks like

Show your team some video clips from Teachers TV (these are free and can be found on the TES website www.tes.co.uk). There is a search facility so you can specify a year group or phase and subject. Although they were made several years ago, some of the issues, such as questioning, pupil engagement and independence, are still very pertinent. They also have a good range on wider school issues, such as bullying and boys' underachievement. These are very useful because you can show just fifteen minutes of film and get staff to comment on what is effective and what they think could be better.

This is a particularly useful tool for working with those staff who think 'I do all that already,' when really you know that their questioning or behaviour management skills could be much better. Often viewing somebody else and reflecting on their practice after discussing it in a department meeting can be a really helpful way of moving on teachers' knowledge about what makes an effective lesson.

Make sure you hand out the current Ofsted criteria for outstanding lessons, too, so that staff are using this to evaluate their lessons, to help them become aware of what they need to do and what their next steps should be.

3. Encourage staff to ask for feedback

Encourage staff to ask pupils for feedback about their lessons: what went well and what could be even better. Or ask them to give pupils a list of five skills in teaching lessons, such as questioning, clear objectives, pupil involvement, challenge and clear instructions. Ask the pupils to rank which areas they think their teachers do best. Look at the following pro forma for an example:

> In lessons, I think my teacher is best at:
> - Encouraging everyone to answer questions
> - Asking questions that make us really think
> - Explaining clearly what we will be learning in the lesson today
> - Giving clear instructions
> - Helping us think about what we have learnt

Don't ask staff to share the results with you, instead ask them to conduct it as research – if lots of pupils tell them that they are good at encouraging them, but asking good questions is further down the list, then this might be an area they could consider developing.

Think about 'marrying up' staff who are trying to work on the same area, perhaps suggesting some *teaching triads* as detailed below.

4. Video feedback

Recent research published by John Hattie in his incredibly useful book, *Visible Learning*[1], suggests that teachers who agreed to watch videos of themselves teach made great improvements in their teaching and improved the achievement of their pupils. Now, I am not suggesting that you whip out the video camera and film all your staff! This needs to be something that they volunteer for and *you* really need to experience being filmed first to see what it feels like! Some of us would probably prefer to have a rusty needle stuck in our eye than watch ourselves on video, because we know we would see ourselves as we really are – I suppose this is why it is so effective! In my mind's eye, I have the hair of Jennifer Aniston and the poise of Helen Mirren, when in reality I know that when I get into my teaching stride my hair looks like a bird's nest and I have the elegance of a short hippopotamus in heels!

I have seen myself on video, and after getting over the awfulness of what I looked like, I did find out some useful things about my practice. For example, my questioning was not as good as it could have been (in fact, sometimes I even answered the questions myself!) and I often neglected to look at the pupils in the very front left-hand corner of the classroom. Although it was undoubtedly cringe worthy to see these flaws in glorious Technicolor, it has helped me improve my

---

[1] J. Hattie, *Visible Learning: A Synthesis of over 800 Meta-Analyses Relating to Achievement*, Routledge (2009).

practice and gain some outstanding observations. If staff are keen to volunteer and you have received permission from your Head, then this can be a useful tool. Of course, it is important to allow the *staff* to view the video themselves to reflect on their practice. Don't share it across the school and certainly don't upload it to YouTube!

5. **Teaching triads**

These are often used in schools to improve the quality of teaching and learning. It involves three members of staff working together to improve their practice in a very specific area. The intention is that it should be a non-judgemental process where small groups of teachers volunteer to encourage each other to refine and reflect on their practice. The focus is on encouragement and any criticism should be purely constructive; this is helped by the fact that all of the members in the 'triad' will be having their lessons observed by each other and are invested in the process.

As an example, you might have three staff who are interested in developing better plenaries to improve the review of learning in their lessons. Perhaps their previous lesson observations have indicated that this should be a target or they are interested in improving this part of their lesson. One of the teachers plans a lesson and her colleagues observe and only report back in a supportive manner on the area of focus: the plenary. They should provide constructive feedback about what went well and mention a couple of ideas about what could be even better.

Then the teachers 'team plan' another lesson, talking about what they hope the pupils will learn and what activities they think will be most effective for this, taking into account the previous feedback. The next teacher teaches it and the other two teachers watch it, give feedback and so forth. The idea is that by focusing on a specific area staff are more likely to make improvements. Furthermore, an observation is not overwhelming and, because of the element of team planning, all of the team have a vested interest in the lesson's success. However, they should be encouraged to experiment and try out different ideas, safe in the knowledge that improvement only comes by taking risks and even making some mistakes. Each staff member should teach at least two lessons that are observed by their colleagues.

The potential to develop improvements by doing this is immense (you will learn not only from the feedback on your lessons but by observing your colleagues, because you have a clear focus and will need to discuss the learning). It does, however, take a large investment of time in arranging cover for not only the lesson observation, but the triad planning and debriefing. I would encourage you to do this, particularly if it is part of a whole school coaching programme or if you can get some agreed cover; trying to shoehorn it into staff's free periods is likely to cause difficulties. It will only be successful if the cycle of observation–coach–plan is followed fully.

If you have your eye on developing your career to the heady heights of the SMT and this teaching triad approach isn't already common practice in your school, you might like to offer your department to trial it out and report back on it to other heads of department who are keen to roll out the process.

Chapter 18

Lesson Observations and Giving Feedback

Observing other people's lessons and giving feedback can be tricky. Lesson observations are an important part of monitoring. We have already seen that we first need to ensure our staff are clear about the success criteria and that we have completed some training or discussion with them in department meetings to address this. Of course, in many schools there are regular whole INSET days dealing with the issue of identifying and teaching an outstanding lesson, and so they might already have a firm understanding about the general theory.

In completing lesson observations across your department, you are really trying to achieve three things:

1. **Knowledge.** Understanding what the current quality of typical teaching and learning is like with your staff.

2. **Identifying areas of weakness.** Whether this is with the resources or equipment that your school or college has or weaknesses in teaching skills, such as in areas of challenge, differentiation or questioning. Identify whether they need improving either as an individual staff member or as a group of teachers or department.

3. **Observing progress.** You have put into place resources or training such as new ICT or you have coached or trained a staff member on an aspect of

their teaching and now you are identifying whether progress has been made. You might also identify some good practice to share across the department.

Remember your role is not as a member of an Ofsted team and although your staff member might request a judgement on their lesson, it can be a very good idea to tell them that you are just going to focus on one area. This has the advantage of giving the staff member a specific area to focus on and is certainly good practice when you are dealing with NQTs or underperforming staff where they might have improved a little in their practice, even if this does not affect the overall grade.

Lesson participation not observation!

When you are conducting a lesson observation don't just sit at the back with a clipboard. Instead, soak in the experience of the lesson. What does it feel like to be in the lesson? How does the teacher interact with the pupils? Are they all engaged and focused on their learning?

You need to skilfully scan the learning area and talk to the pupils about their work. You'll need to pick your moment carefully and try to avoid disrupting the lesson, especially if the teacher is midway through giving instructions or giving a demonstration.

Ofsted inspectors are required to find out from the pupils whether they know what they are learning and to talk to them about learning in the lesson. It is good practice for you to do the same. Ask pupils what they are learning. Ask them what they did in the previous lesson. If they are completing a piece of work, ask them what they need to do to make it good. (This will give you a very clear idea if they have had the learning objectives made clear to them or if they think they are just 'finishing a set task'.)

I often ask pupils about *what* they are learning – asking them to explain it to me. This is a good way of seeing how engaged and interested they are in the learning. Some teachers really try and pull out all the stops when it is a lesson observation in a way that they don't normally. If they are doing group work, ask them if they often work like this. If they are using specific resources, such as mini white boards, do they regularly use them?

Take a look in their books. See how well marked the work is. Ask students if they understand the comments. Look for examples of where pupils have taken on board the teacher's advice – or not. There should be some evidence that the work has improved and that the pupils have actively engaged with the teacher's comments. Remember, *all* pupils need to be making progress. If your data suggests that there are specific groups who are underachieving, such as Gifted and Talented boys, then you would pay particular attention to their learning to see if the lesson is addressing their needs.

Teaching assistants in lessons

If there are teaching assistants or other adults in the lesson, look carefully at how they are contributing to the success or otherwise of the lesson. Ofsted will look to see whether teaching assistants are completing the work for pupils or whether they are encouraging and challenging them to think for themselves. I have been in many lessons where teaching assistants add a great deal to the quality of learning. They rephrase poor teacher instructions; they pose effective questions to pupils and encourage them to think for themselves. However, I have lost count of the number of lessons where I have heard teaching assistants whisper the correct answer to pupils or pick up the pen, completely taking over the piece of work.

In outstanding lessons, pupils need to be developing independence and teachers need to be briefing and working with their support staff appropriately. Sometimes teaching assistants withdraw pupils from lessons and work with them one-to-one. In this case they are actually teaching the pupil so the quality of their teaching is important. If you feel that there might be an issue with the effective use of teaching assistants do discuss this with your staff and your line manager.

In some schools the training given to teaching assistants is sparse and it may be that any concerns need sharing with their line manager (often the SENCO). It may be that teaching assistants require some additional training, as well as a more proactive approach from your staff. If teaching assistants aren't adding value in your lesson it is likely that this is happening across the school, and addressing this across the whole school may be the most effective way forward.

Chapter 19

Five Tips for Effective Feedback

The ability to give good feedback is a skill. I remember from my PGCE days the devastating experience of being given not very good feedback about my lesson in a crass and heavy-handed way by someone completely unsuited to the role of mentor. I felt overwhelmed by the areas that I was judged 'weak' in and was not given any helpful advice about how to overcome these areas of weakness. I remember being told that I had a 'lack of presence' in the classroom and wondering for weeks what this actually meant, what I was doing wrong and where I could get some presence from! How much better it would have been if my mentor had given some specific feedback – when you wring your hands you look nervous; instead put your hands behind your back. Why don't we video you so you can have a look and see what you think and we can discuss it? Or, go and watch Miss Lea teach 9XT; focus on the way she moves and how she issues instructions. Instead, being told I was useless in vague terms just made me feel rubbish and teach even worse – a vicious cycle.

Below are five essentials for giving feedback:

1. Make it prompt!

As a middle leader you probably don't worry too much about having your lessons observed; however, it can be very nerve-wracking for those that you line manage. Before you arrange to observe a lesson work out when you will be giving feedback. Ideally the feedback should be given within the same day, if possible. If you leave it longer than the day after then you aren't being very thoughtful to the person you have observed. They might be finding the experience of having the feedback hanging over them very stressful. On a more practical note, you will be less likely to accurately remember what happened the longer you leave it!

2. Make it private!

Don't get lured into giving feedback in a public place, and if the faculty room is empty when you start and fills up then move! Feedback is private and should not be shared with others. After all, you wouldn't want other people to hear about any failings in your lesson in a public place.

3. Think about how you phrase it

When I started observing lessons I was so keen to tell the teacher what I thought about the lesson that I missed opportunities to really understand the lesson. Yes, the lesson might not have been good, but instead of launching into your comments about its failings, ask a simple question: 'How do you think it went?' This gives the teacher a brief opportunity to reflect. If they say, 'Oh, I realised it wasn't as good as it could be. I was so nervous I spoke for far too long at the start,' this allows you to agree and also makes you realise that they have some awareness about the lesson's failings. It doesn't transform an 'unsatisfactory' lesson into a 'good' one but you can discuss what they could do differently next time, feeling more confident that they realised their mistake. If, however, they say,

'It was a great lesson – there's nothing I'd improve!'
then you know you are going to need to be a little
more focused and detailed in explaining clearly what
its weaknesses were.

4. **Give them a focus**

Don't try to focus on everything. Keep it related to a
few things and this will help your staff make progress.
Questioning and challenge are often useful areas to
look at here.

5. **Appropriate follow-up**

A tearful NQT recently told me that she'd taught a
'rubbish lesson' to her bottom set Year 9 on a wet
Thursday afternoon. Her mentor observed her and
said it was unsatisfactory. She told her NQT not to
worry because she'd watch her again with the same
class next week! How were things going to be different? There are plenty of interventions she could use to
support the NQT depending on the issue with the lesson, from helping her with planning, team teaching or
even boosting her confidence by asking to watch her
with her best class! Watching her again with the same
class wasn't one of them.

You may find that you do have to deal with some staff
members who can't be improved; despite your best efforts
their lessons remain unsatisfactory. Perhaps they refuse
to take advice – this does sometimes happen and you are
advised to talk about this with your SMT link. However,
even if this is the case, you need to do as much as you can
to support and help the teacher improve their practice first,
even if they have been teaching a long time.

Chapter 20

Learning Walks

If your school is working on developing a particular area, such as increasing pupil independence, then using learning walks can be a very effective way to monitor this. The pro forma below is a useful way of dipping into a number of lessons to see what the current status of teaching and learning, behaviour or assessment is and what could be improved. It is also useful to get an accurate judgement of the effectiveness of any interventions you have undertaken, either across the school or within your department.

The intention of a learning walk is that a larger range of classes are sampled than is possible with just a traditional lesson observation. Instead of just focusing on a couple of lessons and observing all of them, a larger range of classes will be dipped into for a much shorter time. For example, perhaps you have been trying to embed independent learning strategies in your department or maybe you have been trying out more active tutorial sessions; you could drop into lessons for ten minutes to observe what is going on – keeping in mind the criteria related to your objective – and then go to another lesson. This would enable you to see parts of six different lessons within a single hour, clearly giving you a much broader range of evidence and the opportunity to see a larger number of classes and pupils. If you have a look at the pro forma below you can see that there is a range of things being looked for here connected to sampling behaviour across a year group by a head of year. You could see which are pertinent in the class you are observing or you could conduct learning walks with another member of staff, each picking different areas to look for.

After conducting a learning walk you will have a body of evidence that you can use to feedback to staff. I would suggest that this is done generally; for example, if you have put into place a new behaviour policy you could talk about the successes as observed by the learning walks and the fact that in eight lessons pupils did not have homework diaries (or whatever the specific focus was for the lesson dipping). It is very helpful to audit current practice and monitor progress as it helps to ascertain exactly what needs to happen next. Learning walks can be a very useful way of monitoring if improvements are taking place effectively and are a very good way of ensuring that complacency doesn't happen, particularly as staff know that you will be following up on issues.

Behaviour for Learning

The purpose of this is to get a broad understanding of behaviour for learning in a range of lessons. The focus of the observation is on the *students* and what they are doing, how they are working. Dipping into a range of lessons at different times will give some indication of the current state of behaviour for learning in the school. The following feedback sheet will be completed.

Focus	Notes
Are students on time to lessons? How many are late? Is this well managed?	
Is the school's behaviour policy displayed? Does the teacher follow the behaviour steps?	
Are pupils wearing the correct uniform. Do they have the correct equipment?	
Do pupils work well in lessons? Do they collaborate well together? Are they well motivated and interested in their learning?	
Any other issues?	

Chapter 21

Lesson Planning: What to Expect

Your school may have a particular format for planning lessons and I would encourage you to use this. Ofsted currently doesn't demand lesson plans when they are observing a lesson but, having said this, I always received one and lessons should, of course, be carefully planned.

A lesson that is carefully planned and neatly typed out doesn't necessarily mean that a lesson will be outstanding. In fact, some lessons that are too tightly planned can be so rigid that the teacher forgets that they can depart from the planned lesson if they realise that it is not achieving its purpose. Seasoned teachers understand the Goldilocks experience and how it relates to teaching lessons. The planned learning needs to be appropriate for all of the individuals in that class and, like the experience of Goldilocks in the bears' beds, it can be 'too hard' or 'too soft' to be effective.

Lesson plans are only a guide about what the teacher might do to help secure great learning in the lesson. A good teacher knows that they need to be flexible about how they use them. For example, a teacher might speed up, miss out or re-teach aspects of the lesson if they realise that the pupils don't understand the topic or if it requires further challenge. Never mark down somebody who doesn't slavishly follow their lesson plan. The best teachers should be constantly reviewing and refining what they are doing throughout the lesson and this often means making changes on the hoof!

We would expect lessons to show evidence of clear planning though – and Ofsted look for evidence that lessons have been well thought out. If a lesson goes wrong or does not have sufficient challenge then looking carefully at the lesson plan can provide a clue as to how the lesson could be improved. Perhaps too little or too much was planned in the time allocated? Perhaps the objectives weren't challenging enough? Perhaps there weren't any objectives at all? Perhaps the timings of the activities weren't sharp enough? Looking carefully at the planning can be useful in helping you to understand a teacher's thought processes and decision making.

What should I expect?

With our teams we would expect them to give us a clear lesson plan which would show that they had spent time considering the class and the learning they intend for them. A lesson plan should have clearly stated objectives, indicating what the teacher intends the class to learn. It should also indicate the ability range of the group and the different types of pupils, such as those on the SEN register, those on the G&T, or EAL. For example, it is common practice to attach a copied page from the teacher's marking records to the plan.

When looking at a lesson plan, one mistake that teachers often make is to focus on the tasks they want pupils to complete, such as writing a leaflet, rather than the *skills* they want them to achieve and master. Be alert to this – good teachers make the learning explicit in the lesson so that the pupils don't think they are just making a leaflet in Geography but know the success criteria for the task.

This helps pupils focus more carefully on what they are learning. It might be that they need to inform residents about what to do in the local area, so it needs to be factual and informative with clear advice about location as well as highlighting to the reader the advantages of the attractions. Many lessons could be improved by a clearer focus on what the pupils should be *learning*, rather than just on what they should be *doing*.

Chapter 22

Work Scrutiny – Under the Spotlight!

In recent years the quality of marking and feedback has become a key issue. This is partly owing to the effect of research collated by the Sutton Trust[1] which highlighted that the most effective thing that teachers can do to help raise achievement is to provide effective feedback and to get pupils actively involved in reflecting on, and responding to, their feedback.

It is also the case that in many schools one of the limiting factors in gaining a 'good' in teaching and learning, and certainly an 'outstanding', is the quality of teacher marking and feedback. It used to be sufficient for teachers to just regularly mark the work, but now the expectations of the quality and impact of feedback are much higher. Work should not just be marked; the feedback needs to be specific and formative, with clear instructive comments that identify where a pupil is doing well and what they need to do to improve.

Furthermore, to be awarded an Ofsted 'outstanding' pupils need to act on this advice, showing that the marking has had an impact on their learning. This might involve pupils responding to the teacher's comments, acting on corrections

---

[1] S. Higgins, D. Kokotsaki and R. J. Coe, *Toolkit of Strategies to Improve Learning: Summary for Schools Spending the Pupil Premium* Sutton Trust (2011).

and showing that they have improved their work as a result of the marking. A recent focus on children's basic literacy and numeracy skills in inspections has also meant that marking in all subjects should address any key literacy or mathematical issues. Teachers should therefore also be involved in marking for literacy and numeracy when this is appropriate.

As a subject leader you will need to undertake regular work scrutiny. If you are a head of year, you will need to ensure that any pastoral programmes are completed effectively. Whatever your leadership role, you will need to monitor the quality of what your team is doing and to act swiftly to address any areas of weakness.

Is monitoring staff really necessary?

Most leaders accept that this is an important part of their role; after all, how will you lead improvements if you are unaware of the current state of play? I have, however, met a few managers who appear to think that monitoring isn't necessary. Once, when I was training some subject leaders and I mentioned the need to conduct marking reviews by looking at books, one middle leader announced, 'I don't need to do that – I completely trust my team!' Obviously I challenged this and explained the need to be accountable for our team's work, adding that monitoring isn't seeking to find fault; it often finds excellent practice and is an opportunity to praise team members and celebrate this.

When I challenged the manager on how she *knew* what the quality of her team members' marking was, her reaction was surprising: 'Well,' she continued, and dropped her voice to a conspiratorial whisper, 'I don't do formal book scrutinies, but sometimes when everyone has gone home … I nip into their classrooms, find their books and look at them then!' Now I don't know about you, but I'd much prefer the middle leader who says, 'Actually, I need to look at your books, it is part of my role; I will want to see class 8x's books in two weeks' time.' The open and transparent process is far better than the underhand leader who says that they trust you yet plans to rifle through your desk drawers when you're not looking!

As leaders we shouldn't feel embarrassed or awkward about the monitoring process – it has to be done and there are ways of doing it effectively.

Whole school monitoring

In some schools the monitoring process will be built into the whole monitoring cycle of the school. These 'marking reviews' will be timetabled in the school calendar and you will be told exactly when to do it: 'All Year 8 books are being looked at in the first week of December.' You will also be given guidance on exactly how to do it: 'Complete the following pro forma on five books per class.' There are clear advantages to this system. If, as busy middle leaders, we were to wait until we had some spare time, it would never get done!

It is ideal if the whole school has an agreed system since this helps you schedule it into your diary and increases its importance with your team. They realise that you are undertaking it at this time as part of a whole school process, rather than as a way to trip them up and check up on them in a mean-spirited fashion.

In many schools, however, it is still up for the subject leader to decide when and how to conduct the review. I can remember, as a new subject leader, being dimly aware that I was supposed to be checking the quality of marking and giving my team notice that I would be checking books the following week. One team member asked if they would receive the books back for the very next Year 8 lesson and without thinking I said, 'Yes.' 'Will you just require a sample of books?' she queried. No, I wanted to be thorough. Every book in Year 8 would be fully examined. What feedback would they receive as staff? Without thinking, I said a full A4 page report per staff member. At the end of the school day, a steady procession of pupils trooped up to my office clutching teetering towers of books and the enormity of the task confronted me. Later in the evening my phone rang – my husband had finally noticed I wasn't home yet – and I was still on the third class set wondering what comment to write on a teacher's marking that said little more than 'wonderful work' with a flourish of a thick red felt pen. This experience taught me a valuable lesson and some tips for conducting marking scrutinies in the future.

Chapter 23

Tips for Conducting Marking Scrutinies

1. Make a schedule

Decide when to see each book/work by year group. Publish this at the start of the year to all staff in your team and remind them what is coming up each term. Try and avoid clashes with main reports and parents' evening when you and your staff will be under the most pressure. Publishing this publically means you are committed to doing this. This is important because as a busy team leader things can easily slip off your to-do list, but keeping to your priorities is important in attaining success. Aim to see a different year group's work each half term. You may be able to dove-tail checking marking alongside some GCSE/A level moderation that you will have to do anyway, so that you don't have to duplicate your efforts. If you have a second in department or person within your team who has a teaching and learning responsibility (TLR) they should also be involved in the monitoring process.

2. Share your expectations

Make sure that all staff understand the marking expectations for your area. Don't presume that just emailing a marking policy is sufficient. You need to discuss it in a meeting to be sure that it is understood and acted upon. Ideally, compile some examples of good marking and feedback and refer to these. You can create a 'best practice' folder with examples of good formative comments and samples of marked pieces. Collect these when you observe some good marking – a photocopy of 'how to do it' and what it looks like in practice is worth a thousand policies. This is a good tool to use with new staff and for setting the standard with your team.

3. Create a pro forma

It is great giving good feedback; I remember as a second year teacher my head of department once telling me how good my marking was and I felt fantastic. It would have been nice to have had this in writing so that I could have used it for my threshold application; however, it can be much harder giving feedback to staff if their efforts are falling well short of the mark.

Creating a pro forma and sharing expectations at the start helps make your feedback much more objective. It can be tricky to tell someone that their comments aren't very helpful; however, if there are set criteria that you are looking for that you have to address when you survey the marking then this really helps both you and them. You can also address any areas of weakness by setting the staff targets for next time. It is also good practice to photocopy this for the member of staff and to keep a record yourself. You will undoubtedly see some excellent practice – make sure you praise the member of staff and ask them if you can take a photocopy of the marking to add to your folder of exemplary marking. This is my form. You can, of course, adapt this or create your own.

Work Scrutiny Form

Date: _____

Teacher: _____

Year Group: _____

Is the work marked regularly?	
Examples of comments that give appropriate advice?	
Are spelling, vocabulary and punctuation errors corrected? (Literacy Across the Curriculum)	
Do the pupils respond to the marking? Does the work show progress over time?	
Areas of good practice to share? Areas of strength in the pupils' work?	
Areas of focus for next time?	

4. **Involve yourself in the process**

You should also ensure that your marking is looked at – this can usually be done by asking your second in department or another team member to look at it. This is good practice, but also shows that you are not exempting yourself from the monitoring process – instead, you are leading by example. Another variation on a work scrutiny can be looking at each other's work in a departmental meeting (this can be useful, but it is by nature much more informal). However, this should not be a substitute for regularly monitoring them yourself. If you lead a very large team and have staff with responsibilities it is a good idea for them to lead specific scrutinies – for example, the Key Stage 3 leader looking at the books for KS3 – however, you will need to monitor the way they do this (there is more detail on this in the chapter on delegation).

5. **Evidence of impact**

I once reviewed a department and the head of department showed me some comprehensive monitoring – she could tell me which team members were outstanding at feedback and marking, and also those members of staff who didn't mark their books adequately. She had completed numerous reviews and these were all well documented; however, although she had given staff feedback, the members of staff that weren't marking the books regularly in November still weren't doing so in June! She had put into place all of the correct systems, but they were not having any effect in improving things in the department. Monitoring is for a purpose: to spread best practice, but also to root out and resolve any underachievement.

Poor markers

If staff aren't marking work regularly there might be a range of reasons – maybe they have been setting a different type of work and this might be entirely appropriate, or they might have been working on paper or planning video presentations for the last two weeks, so don't be too quick to judge. You do need to investigate first before you leap to any conclusions. Perhaps pupils have sat a huge exam, are completing practical work or have completed work in a different form as a display; however, if staff are simply behind with their work or don't expect to have to mark it regularly, steps must be taken to address this.

Remember, it isn't always the lazy teacher who gets behind on their marking, often it is the perfectionist teacher who is always striving to teach the 'ideal' lesson and so gets woefully behind on day-to-day marking, or the newly qualified teacher who thinks that they have to mark every page in great detail. Some staff require support in knowing how to mark effectively or how to set a range of work that doesn't produce masses of marking. Some CPD might be appropriate, such as running a staff meeting on efficient tips for marking, but sometimes if staff just aren't putting in the necessary time to complete their marking then other steps must be taken.

Initially, of course, you need to be supportive and offer suggestions for helping them improve their marking; perhaps they have a very weighty timetable full of GCSE classes who have all just completed controlled assessments. If things are desperate (such as an underachieving NQT) you might even arrange some cover for some of their classes to help them get up to date with their marking, providing a breathing space and some goodwill. But if they are simply not putting in the time necessary to complete their marking then you need to talk through your department marking policy with them on a one-to-one basis.

If you get belligerent staff who feel that marking isn't important you need to challenge their expectations. It can also be worthwhile referencing the Ofsted criteria in the 2014 School Inspection Handbook which highlights that if feedback for teaching and learning is to be effective then there needs to be 'consistently high quality marking and constructive feedback from teachers to ensure that pupils make rapid gains'.[1] Then you need to set a date when you will review their marking again (within two weeks), explaining that you will not be referring the issue on to the SMT on this first occasion, provided it is promptly addressed, but if their marking slips again then you will have to refer it.

It is very important that if your staff member does need some support that you put it into place, whether that's learning some strategies or attending a course on efficient marking. However, if you subsequently find that their marking still hasn't improved then it is necessary to escalate it by discussing it with your senior team leader and asking them to take action.

Pupils don't make good progress if they don't receive regular and effective feedback on their work. If you don't address it, then staff will feel that marking doesn't matter and this attitude can spread across a department. Not marking books effectively can be a disciplinary issue. A phrase that can be useful with stroppy staff who don't like being told that they are lacking is, 'Can I get this right – are you saying that you don't think pupils' books should be marked regularly?' Hopefully you will not have to use this phrase (it is a toughie) but as a last resort it does pull up some staff who argue about how they feel they haven't got time to mark properly. It does usually make them backtrack, but

---

[1] Ofsted, *School Inspection Handbook*, 2014, Ref. 120101.

if they agree with it then you have a clear case to talk to your SMT link and work with them so that the department member gets into line and the pupils get the feedback that they deserve.

Spread best practice by sharing examples of good marking, particularly marking that is effective and efficient but doesn't take hours and hours to implement. Praise staff members who mark effectively and make them feel good about themselves. We all know that, at times, marking can feel very tedious. It takes a large amount of effort; however, there is nothing better than feeling that your actions and efforts have been noticed by your line manager and, more importantly, that your marking is helping pupils improve and make progress.

Whole school marking policy

Your school should have a whole school marking and assessment policy, and obviously it is important that you follow this. It might be that you need to personalise aspects of it to your subject's particular demands: marking in PE and Art are very different to that of English and History. Many marking policies in schools appear to focus on written work, but of course if you are teaching a practical subject or giving verbal feedback this is equally important. You might need to put the demands of your subject in context with the marking policy of your school, explaining how you will set targets or mark work if perhaps you teach practical subjects such as Dance or Drama or Art, if this has not been exemplified in the policy.

Being a subject leader is about ensuring that your team also follows the school party line on marking, so make sure you are aware of it and that your staff are following it. If you are in the situation where your school does not have a marking policy, check with your SMT link; maybe there is one some-where that needs the dust blowing off it and updating by the SMT in charge of assessment. In the short term, if this is an issue then you will be best served by compiling some simple guidelines for your team – ideally a side or two of A4 as guidance for a working marking policy for your department. Looking on the Ofsted website at the subject-specific guidance for your subject might give you some clear ideas about the areas of best practice involved in the assessment of your subject, and the principles below can be used to develop a simple policy yourself. If you have SMT aspirations this is something that you might want to show or offer to use as a basis for a whole school policy.

Creating a feedback policy – some thoughts

- Marking and feedback is given to pupils on a regu-lar basis.

- When pupils receive verbal feedback, where possible they record their actions so they are clear about what the feedback means.

- Pupils understand the assessment criteria and what the teacher will be looking for when assessing their work. Ideally this is reinforced by using exemplar work and setting clear assessment objectives when starting the work.

- Pupils are taught how to self assess and peer assess each others' work. Pupil feedback comments should be recorded with a different colour pen to differentiate pupil feedback from staff marking comments. Self and peer assessment are valuable learning tools – but staff must also look over the annotated work to see that it is being completed accurately.

- Staff will correct common literacy errors where appropriate, in line with the school's literacy policy. Pupils will keep a record of spelling corrections in their homework diaries.

- Not all work requires a mark or level. Pupils do need to be given specific, meaningful comments that indicate what they have done well and what further steps they need to take to improve their work.

- It is expected that teachers will regularly pose questions in their marking or identify specific areas for improvement. Pupils need to be given time to respond to these specific questions, showing that they have understood and have acted on their corrections.

- Pupils' books and folders should show evidence of improvement and progress over time. Pupils should be regularly responding to the specific, effective feedback they receive.

Thinking point

Monitoring is an important part of a subject leader's role. Middle leaders need to know the current standards in their team.

- Do you know the standard of teaching in your team per teacher?

- Do you know the main areas of strength and weakness within the team?

- Have you planned actions to address these areas of weakness? For example, training, sharing good practice, team teaching, coaching, use of external agencies, team planning.

- How can you tell that this is having impact?

- If you have identified any teachers who persistently underachieve, have you given informal support?

- If unsatisfactory performance has continued have you raised concerns with your SMT link? Is there a support programme in place? Does the school's senior leadership take robust steps to address unsatisfactory performance?

- Do you conduct regular marking scrutinies? Do you keep records of these?

- Do teachers receive clear feedback on this marking scrutiny?

- Are the monitoring of marking and the lesson observations having a positive impact on raising the quality of teaching and learning in your team?

- Do you have any CPD learning needs to enable you to do this part of the job?

- Are SMT links effective? Do they help you deal with any staff who do not follow departmental policy and persistently underachieve?

Reflection moment

- What is effective about the monitoring you do?

- What needs improving?

- Do you have any CPD learning needs to enable you to do this part of the job?

What are your next steps?

1.

2.

3.

Section IV

From Monitoring to Measurable Improvements

Chapter 24

Repeatedly Weighing a Pig Does Not Make It Heavier!

As we have seen in the previous chapter, monitoring is an important part of the middle leader's role. We need to know the quality of teaching, learning, behaviour and standards before we can take steps to improve them. Monitoring is a means to an end – that end being exceptional teaching and learning – not an end in itself. We need to use the information we gain in our monitoring of lessons, pupils' work and behaviour around the school to inform us about the next steps we need to take with our department.

An outstanding middle leader does not rest on her laurels. She frequently reflects on what is working well and what could be better. When you are deciding on action to take it is important that you have a sound basis for your decisions. Using the results of pupil surveys, lesson observations, learning walks or book trawls is a way of finding out clear evidence about what is going well and, of course, what could be better. We need to have a clear vision of what we are hoping to achieve and we need to communicate it very effectively to the other members of our team.

Chapter 25

Get SMART!

It's important to have clear priorities for leading improvements. However, I would advise you not to have too many priorities. If you have too many you can feel overwhelmed and end up doing none of them very well. For example, you might decide that you want History to be really popular at GCSE because not many pupils were taking it last year. You need to be specific – it is no good saying that you want it to be more popular. This is far too vague. Be specific – what do you actually want to achieve? When you are thinking about any type of improvement you want to make, be clear and, most of all, be SMART! You want to think about the actual increase, so a better SMART target would be: 'to run two GCSE classes with at least twenty-five pupils per class in September 2015'.

Specific

This is the first rule of the SMART target. How exactly will you know if you have achieved your target? It is important to be clear and unequivocal. It is important that you set yourself SMART targets and use them in your action planning when you set targets for your department, your team members in performance management or yourself.

So don't just be vague – if your NQT says that they want to be an 'outstanding teacher', ask them which specific area they are going to focus on: feedback, or an aspect of classroom practice. Then focus it further still. I saw one action plan where the department head had written: 'Develop better extra-curricular activities for Key Stage 3.' This is far too vague. Being *specific* will lead to a clearer indication of whether you have been successful or not. It also means that if you have not quite met your target, the gap between your intended target and what you have actually achieved will be clear. This can help you see whether it was a slight miss or whether you were far wide of the mark. Think about the target: 'To develop better extra-curricular activities for Key Stage 3 English.' You could SMART this by saying, 'Each year group will receive at least one visit from a writer or poet and/or there will be a writing competition each term.' Or, 'There will be at least one after-school club focusing on each of the key areas of reading, writing or speaking and listening, with at least x members.' By making your target specific you will be much clearer about what you hope to achieve.

One of the issues caused by not making targets SMART is that it can be very difficult to judge whether or not a member of staff has met their performance management targets. If the target is too general, like to 'improve their teaching' or 'improve their marking' or to 'support with the intervention programme at Key Stage 4', then you are going to be beset with problems in evaluating if this has actually happened. Deciding on a clear, unequivocal SMART target will help your staff since they will know what specifically they need to achieve and how they will be judged. It will also stop those awkward reviews where you believe that they haven't really met the targets, but because the wording of them was so vague they feel they can stretch a tiny bit of work into making it sound as if they have actually met the targets. Woolly target setting leads to woolly thinking, leading to conflict between line manager and staff member when these targets are evaluated. It is far better to be specific at the start.

Measurable

The idea of targets being measurable links to the concept of them being specific: is it clear what has to be achieved and is it measurable? Can it be proven? It is about having clear information about whether something has been achieved and to what degree. This could be by numbers – a date by which something has to be done, and subsequently whether it was done at all.

Achievable

Targets need to be achievable and not just dreamed up. Using data and past performance is important here. It is also important that staff members are given enough time to adequately and realistically tackle the project, otherwise it does not become achievable. I remember working with an inept national strategy regional director on a project and they had been over two months late in holding the initial meetings with schools. They had already drawn up an action plan for the group – it was certainly specific and measurable, the only problem being that the actions timetabled for September and October hadn't actually happened because we were having the initial meeting in mid-November! Instead of amending the deadlines in the plan to take account of this, they just announced that all of the September and October work would have to be squeezed into the November actions because the timetable had to be stuck to! Don't do this – it smacks of disorganisation and poor leadership. Your staff will feel like you are incompetent and that you are bringing unnecessary stress into their lives.

Relevant

This is also important. Do targets have relevance for your team? Why do you think these targets are appropriate? What evidence has generated them? The targets you come up with should have a secure basis, otherwise you could find that you are beavering away on something that is not relevant at all – this is a wasted effort.

Making sure that you always make your targets SMART can take a bit of getting used to. It is harder than just summing up vague targets, as you have to think a lot more carefully about the type of targets you are coming up with; however, this is never wasted thinking. Setting targets is important because it is one way of securing improvements for your team. It is like deciding to run a marathon or lose weight. Nobody ever successfully reshaped their body or made a fantastic time at their chosen sport by deciding, 'I am going to run for a little bit sometime next week,' or, 'I am going to get a bit slimmer somewhere in the next two terms.' Instead they set SMART targets: two miles every other day or stopping eating cakes and aiming to lose two pounds a month. You get the picture. Making SMART targets will help you think smarter and sharper. This means that you are much more likely to meet your targets, and of course, recognise that you have been successful once you get there!

Time related

The above action plan was certainly time related – actions had been clearly placed against time – however, there was a massive problem in that some of the months had already passed! Action plans should have dates against them, as this helps you remain aware of what you are doing and when it needs to be achieved by. However, if you do not use a realistic time frame your plans are likely to come unstuck or the crew of your ship may well mutiny!

Action plans

We are clear that our action plans need to be SMART, but we should also make sure we leave time to evaluate them. Very often action plans just relay what we are going to do but we need to reflect on the success or otherwise of a target.

Let me give you an example. You might have an overall target to raise borderline boys' performance in GCSE History by 18 percentage points. You devise some mini targets (SMART, of course) to enable you to achieve this, e.g. to run a series of ten after-school revision classes to be attended by at least fifteen of the targeted borderline boys. The revision sessions should be evaluated as 'good' or better by at least thirteen of the boys – you will issue them a quick survey. You then evaluate this. Maybe you met all of these targets or maybe you didn't – maybe only twelve boys turned up because two were absent; maybe the sessions clashed with English. Or maybe the evaluation highlighted that the boys would have preferred shorter, more regular sessions throughout the year, or that they felt the revision sessions were focused on the wrong topics. Making sure you evaluate what you did gives you the opportunity to plan and comment on what was successful and to learn from it. Evaluation is the key to future success.

Look again at the cycle of improvements diagram on page 47. If there is one thing that really separates outstanding middle leaders from merely competent ones, it is this ability to evaluate the impact of their actions. All too often we have set up a range of projects in response to a need and we are already thinking about the next thing we want to achieve or tick off on our list rather than whether or not it was successful. The ability to evaluate is essential and it is the key attribute in those leaders that are exceptional – whether they are a middle leader, a deputy head or a CEO of a multinational company. When inspecting schools, Ofsted inspectors are given long lists of initiatives that leaders have implemented, whether it is single sex teaching, new courses or methods of teaching – whatever you like. However, the killer question the inspector will always ask is, 'What has been the impact of this initiative?' Doing things isn't enough – you need to be able to evaluate their effectiveness. Don't just think 'I did it'; think, was it worth doing, and how can you show this? What have you learnt from it? Has it actually improved the quality of education for your pupils?

Section V

Managing Change Steps to Success!

Chapter 26

Make It Happen!
How to Manage Change
Successfully

One of the things that really sets apart the outstanding middle leader from the average is their ability to initiate and manage change. Sometimes we don't think about how we manage change very carefully. Often we blunder in thinking we know what we want to have happen and only when it doesn't work out do we think, 'Hey, there could have been a better way of handling this.' And by then it is too late!

I remember as a very green 'would be' subject leader crashing and burning in one interview. It was a job I really wanted, as a second in department. I knew that I was a likely favourite because I had taught a fantastic interview lesson. I had given first rate interview answers about my subject specialism – and I was a GCSE examiner to boot! When I was asked how I would 'go about managing and introducing change' I fell apart and ruined my chances ...

Now I hadn't given 'managing change' a lot of thought because I was naive and very easy to manage as a teacher. When my head of department suggested a new initiative or idea I tackled it with energy and enthusiasm. He was such a skilled leader that his tactics for involving the rest of the department and dealing with less keen members was not immediately obvious to me. I had assumed that, when leading others, everybody would want to do their best; that if I suggested a change I thought was relevant and worthwhile, that they would immediately be behind me – I was wrong! This naivety in answering the leadership questions cost me the job because I wasn't thinking as a potential leader: I was still stuck in the mindset of an expert practitioner. I was very good at being a subject teacher and I expected that all staff would be the same. I hadn't thought about the issues involved in change because I hadn't realised that there would be any: a classic case of unconscious incompetence.

Many people hate change!

Many teachers do not like change. We are creatures of habit. We are used to doing things the way we have always done them. A classroom teacher doesn't have much control over their lives: we are ruled by the bell and an externally set timetable, therefore we find comfort in routine and familiarity. Look around your staffroom – staff like to sit in their own particular chairs, park in the same parking space and drink out of their own favourite coffee mug, and woe betide anyone who stands in their way! Teachers are ridiculously busy people and change always requires additional effort so this can cause some stress. Is it any wonder some people resist change?

So you need to take on board that not everybody will want to adopt the changes you suggest. Not everyone will have the same attitude and beliefs as you. It is really important that you appreciate these two facts. But one thing you can be sure of is that as a middle leader you will have to implement change, whether these are the external changes foisted on us by a government, changes made by exam boards or just the changes and improvements that you can see are necessary to improve things within your own department or area of responsibility.

We can all think of examples in our school or organisation where changes have failed spectacularly, or where planned changes and reforms have quietly withered and died. Either way these are fails, and an amazing middle leader learns from the mistakes of others. If you are to be a great middle leader you will need to be able to manage change effectively. It is a vital skill. This is why you need to think about the *process of change* before you start making any changes yourself. Do this and things will be much smoother, much more successful and your staff will also be much more motivated (even if they still want to sit in the same chair in the staffroom!).

Thinking point

- Think about an example at home, school, or the wider world where change has failed. Why do you think this was? What could the person initiating the change have done differently? What can you learn from this?

- When changes work it can almost appear effortless. But what really happens? Think about a change that has happened in your school or area that has really worked. Why do you think this was? Are there any tips you can take from this successful change process?

- What changes are happening in your sphere of the school? Do you have changing personnel? Curriculum change? Building change? What changes do you want to bring into the school? Why are these important? What will be the benefits for staff adopting this change?

Why change fails

On middle leader training courses when I ask delegates to give me reasons why change fails I can hardly stop them talking! They've all got some 'really frustrating story about a dumb senior manager who really didn't think things through'. They all get very animated and often quite worked up when they relate reasons and tales of why change didn't work and how this influenced their lives in a very negative way. The manner in which they discuss these 'leaders' is often very scathing. A leader who doesn't think through change, one that blunders in and makes everybody's life much harder for very little obvious return, is not easily forgiven.

Teachers often feel that the process of change could have been handled so much better by involving them *before* the change started. Often they know that they could have contributed positively to the change in some way but weren't asked for their expertise or experience. Change can be stressful, particularly if you are a class teacher who is expected to follow through on the change but has had no opportunity to get involved in, or give feedback on, the proposed change. As we have seen, poorly managed change can seriously damage your credibility as a leader and cause important initiatives/developments to flounder and fail. So what can you do to ensure that the changes you propose are effective?

Steps in leading change

First of all, acknowledging that leading change requires some real 'leadership thought' is the first step. Have a look at the following steps and see how considering them can help you lead change more effectively. Remember, the larger the change and the more people involved, the more challenging it can become. If nothing else, thinking about these steps for change is a good idea because thinking and planning for change is the best way to ensure success.

Steps to success

1. **Involve the people that will be responsible for delivering the outcome of the change**

    Get them involved! Discuss the success you require. Listen and plan how to overcome, challenge or support people through any issues in achieving this. Tackling barriers early on will help provide a clear plan of action. Neglecting to consider the challenges involved in setting up a change can doom it to failure. Depending on the type of change, you might want to set up a 'working party', develop a questionnaire for staff or just discuss the issue with a range of different staff, such as NQTs, other middle leaders, experienced staff, etc. Remember, if staff are involved and feel consulted they are more likely to 'buy in' to the change. Also, they may well foresee and predict some issues or offer some insight that will help you make the process of change more successful.

2. **Make the rationale for the change really clear to staff**

    Why is this change or training necessary? How will it ultimately improve things for students/staff? This is important so that there is a 'buy in' to this change and so that staff take on board the messages from the training. Sometimes this is easy because the school or team is responding to external pressures, such as the changes deemed necessary by external forces (Ofsted, examination boards or the government), but if it is an internal decision to adopt a change then people really might need convincing as to why this change is a good idea.

3. Define success

How will you know if you have been success-ful? Sometimes it will be clear cut – at least fifteen additional pupils will have selected Physics A level; attendance will have improved by x%; results will have improved by 8 percentage points – but some-times it is less so. Success criteria need to be as specific as possible to keep you on track and define success. This needs to be shared with the team. Everybody needs to know: what will it look like if we have been successful?

4. Discuss barriers very carefully

Sometimes people are not on board because of vari-ous reasons, including fear, lack of training or feeling that what is being asked is unachievable or will cre-ate additional work. The leader's role is to make it crystal clear why the action is necessary and to ensure that it is reasonably backed up with any supporting information. They must make sure everybody has the appropriate *resources* (including training) necessary to meet the challenge. You can't afford to wait until everybody is okay with the proposed change – you might never get complete agreement, but by looking at overcoming the barriers you will help break down resistance.

5. Be creative in your thinking

You first need to have a solution or end result in mind. Think carefully about how to achieve it. Be time-smart and ask who has done this before you – is there a nearby department? Where is there good practice?

Learn from the good practice of others and avoid their mistakes! Be prepared to use good quality outside help, resources or training on areas you are not an expert in.

6. **Get some champions of change before embarking on a change that will influence and affect everyone**

It can be a good idea to trial it out with a small group who will pilot the project or change. This has several purposes: these staff can 'champion' the issue and become experts in the area; you can encourage them to share their enthusiasm for the change; they can also report back on what works and share strategies with the rest of the staff. It also allows you to trial out the change in a more contained way. If a group of eight staff from different faculties trial out your idea and it needs refining or aspects fail, then this can easily be put right before it is spread to over a hundred staff. Starting small with a group of champions is a wise decision. These champions can help, train or support others in securing the change across the school. Remember, having good champions helps you with developing credibility and spreading good practice.

7. **Clear steps and planning are important to being successful**

Any changes need to be carefully planned for and this plan needs to be constantly under consideration. There should be small, timed, manageable steps for the delivery of the change. Mini milestones should be timetabled in with dates so that there is no unnecessary slippage. Time should be set aside to discuss how well the department is doing at meeting the objectives. Costing and other necessary factors should be added in.

8. Make accountability for actions clear

Is it clear who is going to do things? Do they know? Are they motivated by this? Make sure this is crystal clear and that outcomes and deliverables are specific. If you are devolving responsibility, make sure you allow time to meet and discuss how someone is getting on. Remember: delegating does not mean dumping! (For more information on successful delegation see pages 205–212.)

9. Schedule in time to reflect on the change, individually and as a team

Refer to the plan or change regularly in meetings, and have a plan enlarged and displayed in department areas and in easy reference in your planning. Reporting back on successes is useful in keeping things on track – even something as simple as colour coding, rating items as red, amber or green to show progress. Alterations may need to happen so allow for this; it may be that new priorities need to be added or things adjusted. Adjust and adapt but remember why you wrote the plan and decided on the change in the first place! If something was important then, what has changed to make it less so?

10. Keep mentioning the change

We forget to do things or fail to change behaviour if we are not constantly reminded. Mention the change frequently in briefings, meetings and through emails. Ensure that staff know that you will be evaluating the change and letting them know how it is going. If staff know that you will be periodically checking they are doing something then they are much more likely to comply. Don't just mention something once and expect it to be embedded.

11. **If you find barriers or blockages, discuss them and try to find ways around them**

    If things prove difficult you may need to seek advice from other middle leaders, other schools, or your line manager.

12. **Reflect on the change**

    What has gone well? What could be better? What might still need refining? What could be shared with other areas of the school? You need to be clear about the impact of any change. You should have selected this change because it is important and because it will have a positive impact on pupils and their learning. You need to keep reviewing and reflecting on it so you can discuss how effective it has been.

Reflection moment

Remember, the success of any change depends upon the planning and prior presentation of the change to the team. Make sure you think things through carefully before you start. How will you keep the changes in the forefront of your staff's minds? How many changes are your staff already dealing with? If they are trying to manage too many changes, then these might increase stress: think carefully about which are the most important and don't overload them with unnecessary change.

Section VI

Leading a Team to Success – Avoiding Pitfalls

Chapter 27

The Key to Effective Communication

A good team leader has a very clear purpose and shares this with their team through effective communication skills. We have already discussed the importance of developing our vision, but we need to make sure that we share it. As Chapter 26 on change has clarified, one of the main reasons why change is not successfully embedded in a team or school is because the leader has not articulated its reason or purpose clearly or convincingly enough. In this chapter we will be unpicking some of the strategies to think about in running a team so that your vision is embedded. We will also be considering some of the pitfalls and mistakes that less successful leaders make.

Good communication really is key to running a happy and successful team!

Be available!

We need to make sure that we have some availability for our staff so that ad hoc and casual conversations can flourish. Here you can informally pick up on any concerns that your team might have that require your attention. It also allows and encourages people to share and discuss good ideas.

Reflection moment

- Do I regularly discuss ideas with team members?

- Do staff readily seek me out to discuss ideas – not just to tell me about problems?

- Do I make myself available at specific times so staff know they can find me?

- Does everybody know about the systems we are using and do they readily follow agreed protocols?

- Do all team members contribute in department meetings, including those who are new or inexperienced?

- What strategies do I have to encourage staff to suggest and swap good ideas?

Emails

Email can be an incredibly useful tool; however, it can also lead to misunderstandings, confusion and conflict within teams, so think carefully about how you use it. It can be very useful to convey certain pieces of information: minutes for meetings, reminders of deadlines and sharing resources. However, if you need to talk to someone about something that might be difficult, then doing so face-to-face is really important.

Sending an email doesn't automatically mean that people will do what you say, or even read it! I once worked for a training company who sent so many emails that the important ones were lost among the trivial. Sometimes they would send emails on a Wednesday saying: 'If I don't hear from you by Thursday (the following day!) these are the dates and venues we will be booking for your spring dates.' Just sending me an email with little time to respond didn't mean that I would agree to these requests. When your request has an important implication (here it was the costs involved in booking hotels and printing publicity materials), then speak to someone in person first of all. Needless to say, this company's poor communication means it is no longer in business!

Email doesn't convey your tone of voice or your body language. It can therefore be too easy to misinterpret somebody's tone in an email. Emails at school are sometimes dashed off without the necessary politeness conventions because time is in such short supply. This can mean that a well-meaning email appears brusque at best or even rude to the recipient. I remember receiving one from a deputy head about a forthcoming training event I was running and I waved it under my husband's nose, commenting that she was incredibly rude and that she had a really arrogant tone. He looked at it (there's another disadvantage of emails – they can be easily passed on to other people) and completely disagreed, believing it to be helpful and well meaning, just written in a hurry. He advised me to phone her and see what she said in person. I did and any confusion was cleared up. On the phone she was polite and charming and in person she was even more gracious; however, I had found her email terse and rude, causing me to develop an ill opinion of her.

Remember that as a middle leader you will be dealing with many less experienced or less confident members of staff – you don't want to cause them unnecessary worry and stress. I once ran a series of training sessions for a school and discussed how poor use of email by leaders created stress. This really rang a bell for one middle leader, who explained that she had received an email from the deputy head (her line manager) on a Friday afternoon saying that he 'really needed to talk to her on Monday morning about something'. This hard-working and very conscientious head of department had spent much of the weekend worrying about what it could be and what she had forgotten to do. When she spoke to the deputy head on Monday, her fears were unfounded – he had really sent her the email to remind himself that he needed to talk to her! And far from it being a negative issue he wanted to talk to her about some additional funding he had secured and to ask her if she had any ideas about how to spend it! Here he should have outlined what it was he wanted to discuss with her: 'Just a reminder, Gill, I need to catch you on Monday because we've got an extra pot of money and I know you'll have some good ideas about how to spend it!' He should have made it sound low key – or not even sent the email at all!

So think carefully about how you use email and what its purpose is, and remember, never ever send an email in anger or after a few glasses of wine – I've done it and I've lived to regret it!

Chapter 28

Meetings and Messages

Meetings can be very useful mediums for passing on key messages. However, most team leaders don't feel that they have sufficient time to meet with their team and therefore it is important that these meetings don't just become an information giving session! You need to use some of the meeting time to secure and improve practice and lead changes in teaching and learning or the specific area that you are leading on.

Some ideas that successful middle leaders have employed to pass on administrative information effectively include the following (but be selective – don't use all of them!):

- **Whiteboard**

    Putting up a large whiteboard in the department area whereby written reminders for the week can be easily displayed.

- **Weekly Bulletin**

    Making a yellow A4 sheet for the week with reminders on it, including deadlines, assessment information and information about visitors, highlighting new resources and messages from other meetings. This yellow sheet can also be easily referred to by staff and it can be emailed too. It means that communication about key information can easily be managed. It also means that people do not keep asking you the same questions – 'When was it that Year 9 reports are due?' or, 'What is the title of the new assessment?' You can refer them to the yellow sheet. Ideally try and keep it very brief and clear so that it keeps to its purpose and becomes a very useful weekly bulletin. It might be appropriate to add in a resource or website of the week too. The time spent creating this (and you can ask for admin assistance) will be easily repaid because you won't be repeatedly stopped or interrupted to be asked the same thing. It is also very useful in helping part-time members of staff keep up to date. You should ask other members of staff for dates and information updates that they wish to include.

- **Weekly stand-up briefing**

I make an annual visit to a school to run GCSE revision sessions with their Year 11 pupils. Since it is an epic journey from my house I always try to arrange the visit for a Friday. This benefits the pupils as it is a fresh face at the end of the week (it also benefits me because I can recover from the journey on the Saturday). I have noticed that every Friday the head of department runs a short feedback session on 'wins' of the week, summarising what has gone well and celebrating the good things that have happened. One member of staff is awarded a bottle of wine or another inexpensive 'feel good' treat for some valued contribution they have made to the team and there is much laughter and good cheer. There is also a brief reminder of what is happening the next week and what people need to remember to get done, e.g. reports. It takes less than ten minutes. It is a very large department but everybody seems happy and up to date and every year I secretly want to be working in that team (the only problem being the five-hour commute from my house!). There is a lovely, purposeful atmosphere created by a positive head of department who is a great communicator and motivator!

• **Monthly or weekly department lunches**

Everybody signs up earlier in the week to bring something to share, such as bread, cheese, salad, cold meats, or crisps, and everybody shares and chats. If you have a very small department, even just deciding to eat your lunch together on certain days could be a good idea. In one team I worked in there were five of us and we formed a 'Sandwich Club'. Everybody took turns to make sandwiches for the team. I made them on Monday and knew that for the rest of the week I would have some delicious freshly made sandwiches ready-made for me: team building and time saving! (There was an agreement that unpopular fillings such as egg and tuna were never used.) I left that school over thirteen years ago but I hear that the Sandwich Club is still going strong, with all new members!

Running meetings

Having been in a school for a few years you will probably have sat in more than a couple of useless or badly run meetings. You will therefore be aware of some poor practice that can occur when running meetings. This might include using rooms that are too small, too cold or too hot; not having any refreshments; or overrunning by half an hour or more. It could be that the manager does not communicate the agenda in advance of the meeting so people are unsure whether there is a meeting or not and they are unable to prepare effectively.

A great team leader makes sure that the meeting is relevant to all members of staff or arranges the meeting in such a way that it benefits all members. Perhaps you need to discuss A level matters but three team members do not teach A level, so you would be thoughtful if you had this agenda item last, so that those who were not involved could be released early from the meeting.

Do remember to ask any staff if they have any other business in advance of the meeting. If your Key Stage 3 manager wishes to discuss the finer points of Year 9 assessment and this is likely to take at least twenty minutes then this should be a main agenda item, rather than an add-on. You don't want to be shanghaied by lots of additional items that could cause you to lose control of the meeting as the agenda overruns.

Good meetings

Good meeting practice involves ensuring that the right agenda items are included. Circulate any reports or reading material before the meeting and ensure that you tell people the meeting time and venue. If you have other team members who are taking leadership roles, then they are likely to want to make contributions too. It is a good idea to not make the agenda overlong. You might find it useful to put alongside the agenda item how long the item will be discussed for – this can be a useful way of keeping things on track. So item 1 might read:

Feedback on main issues from Year 11 mocks
(20 mins) ELO

It is also important to give the initials of the person who will be leading this part of the meeting and to discuss their contribution with them beforehand. I've been embarrassed in meetings before by the leader turning to me and saying, 'Caroline, you are the next agenda item,' when I have been completely oblivious to this fact. I can't have been the only one to have been caught out in this way. If you expect somebody to lead part of the meeting always ask in advance!

A good meeting should have clear outcomes and feel like a worthwhile use of people's time. Think about whether people have got involved in the meeting. Was it just an information giving session and, if so, was this the most appropriate means?

Finally, a meeting shouldn't just be the team leader dictating items. It does happen, but if you want your team to 'buy in' to your ideas you need to not only allow them to have a voice, but to be interested in hearing what they have to say. A great leader knows that they don't necessarily have all of the answers. In a good meeting everybody should get the opportunity to contribute and feel involved.

Minute taking

Somebody in the team or an admin support needs to take the minutes of the meeting. It is ideal if these can be recorded straight onto a laptop as this saves the secondary job of typing them up. Ensure that the minutes state the date, who was present, who sent apologies and what was discussed. Good minutes should have a clear record of what was agreed and a clear follow-up column where it indicates what the outcome will be and who is responsible for ensuring its completion. This is important because it means that in the subsequent meetings these minutes can be referred to, and it keeps track so that actions that are agreed on are followed through. At the start of the next meeting the minutes should be referred to and agreed. It is also good practice to forward the minutes and agreed actions of the meeting soon afterwards to all those in attendance and those who gave apologies – your line manager may also ask to see them.

Section VII

Training and CPD

Chapter 29

Make Training Count!

I run courses for many hundreds of teachers every year. I notice that some delegates make notes avidly and ask me questions while others seem much less concerned with retaining the training information and instead seem set for a fun day out. When I ask the keen ones why they are at such pains to make careful notes, they often mention that they need to do something specific with the training, such as using it to train others or refresh the curriculum, or they have been asked by their heads of department to feedback five key things from the training to the department in the next meeting.

Training is expensive and you want to make sure that it has a positive impact, so I would urge you to make sure that your team members know that they will be required to do something with it after the event. CPD opportunities are usually required as a result of the performance management process, but education is always changing and new opportunities or attractive looking courses might mean that team members request to go on some training that hasn't been pre-planned. If they do attend, make it clear *before* they go that they will be required to feedback to the team. This might be a 'mini teach' of the course in twenty minutes, or even just sharing the top five ideas that they have taken from the course. This should be the case even if it is just an NQT going on a course about 'How to make French grammar more engaging'. We have all got something to learn from others and allowing staff to go on CPD is expensive in terms of both time and money.

Once staff know that a day's training in London will mean that they have to do something meaningful with it, then it will deter those who just see a course as a jolly day out. Good CPD is not just a chance for a trip to the nearest exciting city for a day in a posh hotel! Adopting feedback practice will ensure that staff are really committed to the training, that they stay alert to the end of the course and that your whole team can benefit from the day.

Where to find training courses

Most staffrooms are choc-full of multi-coloured fliers but, if not, a quick search online should provide plenty of ideas. You can receive training from several training companies,[1] your subject associations, your Local Authority or academy networks. If you are planning to put staff on a new course and you are unsure about the company, ask them to send you copies of previous course evaluations and try to get some good 'word of mouth' feedback from teachers who have attended the courses.

Remember, a good training day isn't just about the hotel and speaker, it is also about the number of people on the course – are there usually hundreds of people or very small groups? A shy teacher might like to hide in a large group, but if you are hoping for some individual interaction with the trainer then a smaller number is preferable. A good

---

[1] Try Teachology-education.co.uk for a range of exciting day courses and useful conferences with a range of different speakers. Or try Osiris Educational (www.osiriseducational. co.uk), a very well-established training company.

company will have no hesitation in providing you with this information.

Thinking point

Some questions you need to be able to answer regarding arranging CPD for your staff include:

- Do you identify CPD requirements as part of the performance management system?

- Do all staff, regardless of their experience, receive the opportunity to refresh their practice?

- Is the CPD arranged for staff the most effective for their needs?

- How do you ensure that CPD has an impact on staff's practice and that it really benefits pupils?

- Do you receive a range of information about appropriate courses, books and other CPD activities?

Reflection moment

- **Do you know how to request CPD for your team?**

  Some schools have a central system whereby requests from team leaders are passed to the deputy head (who oversees the budget). In other schools you will be devolved a larger pot of money and you are expected to make good use of it. You might need to factor in travel costs, as well as supply cover rates, so make sure you ask before you start booking things.

- **Are you creative in your use of CPD?**

  You need to think creatively about how you arrange CPD and how you get best value. Some top daily courses cost in excess of £300; add to that cover and travel and you could be looking at close to £500 for a one-day course for just one individual! Sometimes it is most effective for an *individual* to go on a course, especially if it is something that is specifically tailored to their individual needs, such as 'Business Studies for NQTs' or 'Course for New Middle Leaders'. Also, staff sometimes receive a much needed morale boost from meeting other teachers in a similar situation who are tackling similar issues. As a middle leader yourself, for example, it would be of real benefit for you to attend some external training so that you can think strategically away from the hurly-burly of school.

- **Eight for the price of one!**

  Some effective middle leaders think more creatively about using their budgets and this is important if you have several team members facing similar issues. You might want to organise a twilight or after-school session for *all* members of staff. See if you can get last lesson covered too, throw in some nice sandwiches or a pub meal afterwards and get everybody trained at the same time. You can even invite department members from some other local schools and ask them to make a contribution towards the cost.

- **Tailored training for your team?**

  Sometimes getting an exam board representative, an advanced skills teacher (AST) from another area or an independent external consultant in for a couple of hours of focused training can be just what's needed. You can ensure that all of your staff hear the same messages and this is important for following things through and developing consistency across the team. Although you might think getting an external speaker in will be prohibitively expensive, you will probably find it is much cheaper than sending a couple of staff on an external course. You can also ask the trainer to tailor the session exactly to your school's requirements. Make sure that you pick a really good trainer – it's advisable to choose one that you have already heard speak or who has been recommended to you. You should also check whether their fee includes transport and accommodation or whether you will receive an additional bill for this, otherwise you might be in for a nasty shock!

Section VIII

From Rock Star to Honey Bee

Chapter 30

How Not to Lead a Team!

In Chapter 6 we looked at some of the characteristics that effective team leaders share. Looking in more detail at how to lead a team, we realised that the way we act and the way we are perceived by our team really affects our success. Individual team members' opinions of us and our actions will influence how far they are ready to engage with us as a leader.

Instead of listing a huge amount of information about the different things a team leader can do to inspire or annoy their team, it is perhaps more effective to consider some of the 'types' of leaders in schools and other organisations. Although the following are perhaps exaggerated versions, they do highlight some of the very real mistakes that team leaders make. We can learn from these errors in habit and behaviour so that we are more effective and become better leaders.

I have given each of these four leader types a name, and I shall first introduce you, with a flourish of applause and the sound of the bass guitar, to the Rock Star middle leader!

The Rock Star

Can be identified because:

- They see leadership as being all about them! They make a big fuss about their title, displaying it on badges/ desks/doors/excessively long footers in emails (they might even be ridiculous and spend school money on personalised compliments slips and business cards! Don't ever do this – it smacks of having an ego and budget much larger than your brain, and a good bursar will question this spending big time!)

- Being a middle leader is all about their ego; it's about being seen to be important and amazingly fantastic at all they do. They appear to have lost sight of the fact that they are heading up a team and, like a lead singer in a rock band, try and take all the glory (and photo opportunities) for themselves. They can easily be spotted because, when talking about the department, they use 'my' and 'I' rather too much: 'my Geography department', 'in my classes', rather than 'we'. They are often very good teachers, sometimes even outstanding – but they think too much in terms of *their* classes, and *their* results rather than the department as a whole.

Rock Stars are poor leaders because:

- Rock Stars often come crashing down when their department is externally evaluated because although their own practice might be very good, they have not paid sufficient attention to the needs and concerns of others. Rock Star middle leaders make poor interviewers because they often do not want to pick the best candidate for the job – they feel threatened if they are not the very best in their team. Instead they are looking for a new, dewy-eyed groupie who will agree with what they say and give out good ideas that can be repackaged as their own, while also providing constant adulation and endless cups of tea!

- Rock Stars have far too great an ego to make good leaders. Sometimes they secretly suffer from a lack of confidence which they cover with a thin veneer of swagger. Team members do not flourish under a leadership which is run by an egomaniac and these departments often have a very high turnover of staff, or are filled with new, very impressionable staff. Rock Stars have some positives in that their own practice is often very good, but they have not learnt that they need to develop and encourage others. Often they realise (or others soon realise) that they are unsuited to their middle leader role, although sadly some of them do move on to become SMT, which further inflates their sense of grandeur. They can also be found running external consultancies (fulfilling their Rock Star ambitions by calling these training courses 'gigs' on Twitter) or they may become ASTs (another role for which they are wholly unsuited). A good AST is an expert practitioner but they see their role in coaching and developing others to share their good practice.

Being in a Rock Star's department is very frustrating, but it is hardly any better being in the Honey Bee's department.

The Honey Bee

Can be identified because:

- The Honey Bee – or Queen Bee to give her the title she more aptly deserves – shares several characteristics with the Rock Star leader. Essentially she is also rather too concerned with herself; however, she can be quite charming and amiable and her egoism is hidden under a beguiling layer of sweet honey. Many people have inadvertently found themselves working for a Honey Bee and when I say working, I mean working!

- Honey Bees often look incredibly busy. They buzz around the school, often looking immaculate in outfits from Monsoon and NEXT, holding folders and looking important, scrolling on their Blackberries. However, this is an act (and one that we can learn from: carrying multiple folders, even if they are empty, makes you look busy!). The fragrant Honey Bee isn't that busy as she has a hive full of workers doing all the jobs that she doesn't want to do! And this is the real sting in the Honey Bee's tail – she doesn't want to do any hard work herself and, worse than that, she wants to keep all of the honey for herself.

Honey Bees are poor leaders because:

- They keep all of the 'honey' for themselves and this means that they are essentially selfish. Selfish people don't make good leaders. What the honey is depends on the Honey Bee – whatever it is they most prize. It might be taking the chief share of the A level teaching (when there are others keen to have the opportunity to teach it), or it might be arranging the timetable so that they are never ever scheduled to teach on a Friday afternoon or so that they *always* get top sets for GCSE or the best teaching room (even if it means their poor NQT trekking back and forth across the school!). The issue with the Honey Bee is that they are always looking out for themselves first and this means that other team members in the hive become increasingly demotivated. This might be because they receive far too many lower sets/difficult tasks or responsibilities. What the Honey Bee doesn't realise is that while she is having an easier time of it her exhausted staff see right through her!

- Working for a Honey Bee is also demotivating because you find yourself doing an excessive amount of work for very little reward. If you start thinking that you might have 'Honey Bee tendencies' then nip these in the bud – after all, remember what happens in a real hive in a garden. After several summers of sweating and collecting nectar for the queen bee, the worker bees decide that it is time for a new queen! One of the ways they get rid of the old queen bee is to essentially hug her with their wings, suffocating her to death. If you think you might have been 'queening' it over your team for a while and you've had more than your fair share of honey, when your team suggest a 'group hug' don't say you haven't been warned.

Remember: a good team leader does her share of the hard graft and always shares out the honey!

While being a Honey Bee is a definite mistake, going too far along the other end of the spectrum is also one. The Martyr is a role that some well-meaning middle leaders fall into, often as a knee-jerk reaction to having been managed by a Honey Bee or a Rock Star.

The Martyr

Can be identified because:

- Martyrs have the best of intentions; however, it is not a management style you should try and emulate. Often Martyrs have experienced being managed by a greedy Honey Bee who has taken all of the honey and glory for themselves.

- Martyrs are good people – they remember what it is like to be overlooked and undervalued by their previous leader so they resolve never to do the same to others. They are determined not to be unfair. You won't find a Martyr keeping all of the honey for themselves – far from it. If you work for a Martyr it can initially be quite refreshing. You will find that you get your share of the easy classes and they are always looking out for you. If you look a little peaky, they will do your breaktime duty for you, offer to mark some of your mocks, and will happily supervise your after-school detention.

Martyrs are poor leaders because:

- Martyrs can appear to be good leaders but their well-meaning intention to be fair and helpful to others becomes twisted into a situation where they fail to give themselves a decent enough deal. Whereas the Honey Bee is selfish in that they keep *all* of the honey for themselves, the Martyr does the opposite. He or she is so keen that their department sees them as fair that they overcompensate. They give themselves the most difficult classes for *every* year group. They teach in the worst rooms and their overriding desire to make things easy and pleasant for their colleagues means that they end up with a terrible deal, all of the time!

- This often leads to Martyrs losing their sparkle and enthusiasm and they can appear resigned, jaded, and even a little moany. You don't want this in a leader. A good leader needs to enthuse and inspire others! The Martyr will often propose something in a meeting and, when nobody rushes forward to do it, say with a sigh, 'Oh well, I will do it – again!' Their immediate reaction is one of wanting to solve things and smooth things out for their department members, which can lead them to allow their department members to become lazy and complacent: 'Oh well, Kate will fix it,' or, 'It won't really matter if I miss the deadline, Mike will understand.' This sort of attitude is not one that should be allowed to take root in a good department. Looking out for your team members and supporting them is one thing – babying them and letting them absolve themselves of their responsibilities as a class teacher is another!

Remember: an effective leader allows themselves their fair share of the good stuff too! If you entirely forget about your needs you will become grumpy and depressed. A good leader helps people to solve their problems rather than launching in and doing it for them.

Finally, look across to the far corner of the staffroom and you might catch a glimpse of the Zombie leader. This leader needs to be looked out for early on in the school day because by three thirty they will have left the building and shuffled off home.

The Zombie

Can be identified because:

- They are likely to have been in their post a long time, sometimes a very long time. They would be exceptionally unlikely to get a middle leadership post these days because any verve or enthusiasm has long since departed their bodies. They are like the proverbial zombies from 1950s horror films: automatically, woodenly sleepwalking their way through their job. And the danger with them, like the zombies, is that they will spread their mind-numbing dullness and energy-sapping malaise, infecting all those they encounter. Their cynical world weariness turns even the sparkiest NQT into a dull-eyed automaton. Their classrooms are often very disorganised, dusty and untidy, rammed full of ancient resources that might one day 'come in handy'.

Zombies are poor leaders because:

- The Zombie has long since lost any real interest in the role of head of department or head of year. Their glazed eyes are fixed unblinkingly on the hazy horizon of retirement or a post in another school (they never get it or even get round to applying for it!). They have neither the will, enthusiasm or energy to lead their department with any success.

- Zombies carry on doing things the way they have always done them and hanker after the teaching of yesteryear when it was all about chaotic but charismatic teaching where the hard-working pupils passed and those that didn't, well, it wasn't your problem. The Zombie has stopped struggling and defending their department against all of the initiatives of the new perky assistant head teacher; instead they smile a half smile, shrug and trudge on doing things the way they always have.

- Sometimes the Zombie's lack of leadership is covered up by the work of a bright and enthusiastic junior team member who strives to improve things, working around them and taking control of what needs doing. If there's a Zombie heading the team (with no backup) then there is frequently a high turnover of staff because the team lack direction and the Zombie's lack of interest in leadership means it becomes very difficult for the everyday teacher to do their job effectively. Occasionally there may be an internal coup as a frustrated second in department tries to take up the reins, particularly if the department has been identified as inadequate by Ofsted or a new head teacher realises that they are blocking progress. Zombie leaders are, of course, to be avoided at all costs because they will bring down the morale and enthusiasm of any team – and nothing will get done.

Hopefully reading this you will realise that you are neither a Rock Star, Honey Bee, Martyr or Zombie. However, be alert to some of the tendencies and pitfalls that each type of leader brings. Maybe you are incredibly high achieving and seek the best with your classes and you need to keep these high standards but ensure that you don't allow yourself to get all 'Rock Star'. Perhaps you can feel yourself wondering if you should just do it yourself again, with the world weariness of a Martyr – either way, keep these tendencies in check.

Section IX

How Team Members Know
that You are a Great Leader

Chapter 31

Ten Traits of Great Team Leaders

Teams look for great team leaders who:

1. **Always act fairly**

   You will like some staff members more than others and some will be better than others, but you need to always act fairly. If you have relatives in the same department then make sure you can't be accused of nepotism – staff will feel undermined if they feel that major decisions are discussed at home rather than at work!

2. **Do what they say they are going to do – when they say it!**

   Be known for being someone who follows through on promises.

3. **Champion the cause of the department**

   While you don't expect a great leader to go head-to-head with the SMT all the while, you would expect them to be proactive and assertive in highlighting and championing your department's cause to the rest of the school. Your middle leader needs to ensure that your team gets a fair deal.

4. **Are organised**

They know what is happening and they ensure that this is communicated clearly and easily to others.

5. **Look up and see the bigger picture**

They use their knowledge to predict where problems might occur and they know what to do about them, ideally before they become a big problem.

6. **Are interested in you as an individual and as a teacher**

They are keen to know that you are well and happy. They make it their business to know your strengths and how you hope to develop in your class teaching or your career. They encourage you to develop and progress.

7. **Make things happen that will benefit the pupils and the department**

Whether it is securing additional funding, dealing with difficult pupils or ensuring that everybody has the resources and training needed to enable them to do their job efficiently, they make it happen.

8. **Listen**

They know that you have good ideas too. They take these on board. They know that other people might have the answers and if they do they don't steal them and attempt to take credit for them!

9. **Appreciate you and others**

They say thank you frequently and mean it!

10. **Are a good role model and really walk the talk**

Their everyday actions actually reflect their values and the aims of the team.

Section X

The Important Art
of Delegation

Chapter 32

Factors Involved in Good Delegation

 It is only as we develop others that we permanently succeed.

Harvey Samuel Firestone

Do you delegate or do you dump? If you have ever had tasks just dumped on you, you will know that it isn't a great sensation. However, the ability to effectively delegate is a skill that a great team leader has mastered. Getting it right can make the difference between people contributing willingly or getting huffy.

So, there are three likely delegation scenarios. Firstly, that you have at least one person in your team that you can delegate to. Ideally they are in a paid position with an additional teaching and learning responsibility. This is helpful because here when you delegate you are actually only allowing them to undertake a key part of their role and they are getting paid for doing this! However, just because somebody is being paid to take on additional responsibilities, it doesn't mean that they always enter into these with any great enthusiasm. You will still need to manage them effectively to ensure that the tasks get completed to a good standard and that they are always on their radar. Working with other staff, whether it is your second in department or key stage coordinator, your challenge is to ensure that individuals complete their paid responsibilities to a good standard and that their actions show impact.

No one to delegate to?

Secondly, you have nobody to delegate to but you can use 'favour delegation'. It may be the case that the other members of the team do not receive any extra payment or allocated time for undertaking extra duties. Maybe there is nobody who can be directly expected to share the workload with you. Here's where the 'keenies' might come in. There are often some 'keenies' who you might be able to encourage to help out with things – even if they are only in their first few years of teaching or even on their PGCE or training.

If you don't have somebody specific to delegate to within your department then this can be a lifesaver! This is 'favour delegation' though, and you do need to think very carefully about how to encourage such staff and make the tasks attractive to them. Hopefully you can motivate staff with the phrase, 'This will be great career development.' Naturally, when you are encouraging staff to help you out, rather than managing them doing aspects of their paid job, you need to really think and discuss with them what areas they are interested in. Delegation here is them doing you a favour because they want to. So make 'em want to!

Think and talk to them about what they are interested in and explain how completing this task will help them, whether that's furthering their career, learning new skills, allowing them to extend their interest in the subject or just making them feel part of the team. You will be able to delegate much more effectively if you make it fun and worthwhile for them!

Recruit 'givers'

Don't forget that when you are interviewing staff this is a great opportunity to get them to show their interest in taking on additional aspects, particularly running extra-curricular clubs. A few judicious questions about what they would like to contribute to the department, and what their skills and enthusiasms are, will help you to identify if you will have willing helpers in the future or not! If you are choosing between two similarly qualified and suitable candidates for a main scale post, then the candidate that might be able to offer something extra or be a willing volunteer is the one that might well have the edge. Make sure that you don't overemphasise what 'extra' they can offer though, as it could be rather off-putting! It is more about spotting people's talents, aspirations and aptitudes to help out and providing them with a way of developing these, whether that's running an after-school club or developing new schemes for Year 7.

No one at all?

Thirdly, you might well be the lone person who is responsible for this area in your school. You might be the sole music teacher or lead coordinator for RE. Maybe there is nobody you can delegate to, directly or indirectly. Maybe you have a staffroom full of cynics and all the new teachers are struggling with their role – it is your job and it is just you that has to do it!

If this is the case then don't despair; however, you will need to get busy networking and finding out other ways of getting ideas and assistance with sharing the load (look again at page 85 where we discuss five fabulous connections). *Remember: a good leader gets things done and doesn't necessarily have to get it all done themselves.* It might be the case that there is nobody in your school who you can officially delegate to, but who says that you can't borrow ideas and expertise from other schools, other leaders or even from online forums? Even without somebody to delegate to, you can make effective use of other people's skills, ideas and time to help you get things done.

Thinking point

Think about a time when somebody delegated something to you and it went well. You felt motivated about it and were pleased to do the task. It could be in school or in your home life. What was it about the delegation that made it effective? Why did you feel motivated to undertake the task? What made you want to do it?

Steps in effective delegation

Here are some things to think about when you are delegating a task to someone:

Why are you asking them to do it? Is it part of their job? Is it part of their role and responsibility?

One of the ways in which middle leaders get overloaded by jobs is that they struggle to ensure that other staff who have paid responsibilities actually follow through on these. Often staff with responsibilities have not been given clear enough job descriptions; if you think that this is the case you might need to revisit this with your SMT link. Or perhaps their job description is accurate but they are not getting actively involved in following it!

Imagine that I have a Key Stage 3 coordinator and I want them to get actively involved in primary/secondary transition. I would need to have a discussion with them about this to ensure that we were both clear about what was involved and how this related to their role.

Some points to consider include:

- **Am I being clear about what the outcome is?**

    I need to outline what the task is and explain why it is important; people often do not take enough time to do this. Regarding the idea of improved primary/secondary liaison, it would be wise to evaluate what is already happening, if anything. I could ask my second to find out what staff in both schools think is already working well and what could be better. You might even like to do a SWOT analysis about it with the coordinator (see pages 53–55 for details on completing this).

    It would be wise to ask your staff member (or gently direct them) to find out what best practice is, either locally or nationally, and plan to address some specific areas.

- **Give ownership to the other person, but make the parameters of the task clear.**

    One of the worst things about having a task delegated to you is if you are micromanaged to a ridiculous degree by your line manager. You do need to ensure that they are clear about what you would like them to achieve and what the parameters are. However, if you micromanage every last detail you might well find that they become demotivated by the task – after all, if they can't include their own ideas they might as well let you do it!

    A wise primary head teacher who was very skilled at leading others once told me, 'If I want somebody to take over a task I give them the parameters: what is essential and what is non-negotiable. But after this I let them have some freedom. If there is an ideal way that I want it done, an absolute blueprint, then I do it myself – otherwise it is not fair.' I think that this is a good rule of thumb when you are delegating to others.

It is really important to make the parameters of the task clear to the person you are delegating to because they shouldn't be playing 'guess what is in my head'. Imagine how demotivating it would be to invest a lot of time and effort into completing something that might be completely unsuitable, then being asked to do it again! Be very clear about your parameters and don't have too many. People are most motivated if they feel that they are allowed to come up with their own ideas and if the task stretches and engages them.

Action planning and SMARTs

Make sure that the person undertaking the task under-stands the parameters and, if it is a big task or project such as a Key Stage 2/3 transition project, ask them to complete an action plan. Remember, effective action plans are clear about what they hope to achieve. They give time milestones for actions, indicate likely costings (in terms of time and money) and they clearly note who is responsible for each action. They should also have space to allow the action to be evaluated after it has happened. How successful was it and what was the outcome? What was the impact of the actions? This act of planning helps them with a project or task because it encourages them to think about the stages involved in the project. It also gets them to plan for the impact and evaluation and gives them the opportunity to think about costing, whether it involves cold hard cash, cover money or both! It is important that this is considered. It is no good asking them to think about extra-curricular enhancement for more able Key Stage 4 students across the school if they don't know whether they have a budget of £50 or £5,000! It is important to get staff to plan even if they are super keen because the act of planning allows them to think things through properly and consider what they hope to achieve. It also addresses the issue of some keen members of staff who start lots of initiatives but don't follow them through sufficiently.

Make sure that you don't delegate things to staff that are far beyond their understanding or skill set. You will want to stretch and challenge staff, but you don't want to overwhelm them.

Check in regularly

Once somebody has agreed to do a project or task, make an agreement for when you are going to 'check in' with them, ideally giving them a date. This is really important. You need to hear how they are getting on, and also give them the opportunity to talk about any emerging issues they have before they threaten to derail the project.

Having a check-in discussion allows you to still keep a handle on what is happening and ensures that the project or task does not drop off the radar of your team member. In school everybody is so busy that even the most diligent of us can be guilty of allowing a project to slip. You don't want this to happen, so when you are setting up the delegated task, agree on a reasonable time and a date for a follow-up and make sure it happens. It need only be a brief discussion. As the middle leader you still have ultimate responsibility for the action you have delegated and you don't want to find out hours before the Year 6 transition day that your second in department has totally forgotten to arrange anything for the MFL department!

I used an exercise book with one second in department where we would chart the actions that had been done and note down any next steps. Just glancing at this in a meeting would remind us of what had happened last and what the agreed actions had been.

Feedback and thank them

Remember to ask somebody who has completed a task for you to reflect on how it went. What went well? What was harder than anticipated? How well did you delegate to them? Get some feedback. Don't forget to say thank you either – if someone has put in additional time for you, it is really important to appreciate it. Whether it is just a quiet word, a card in their pigeon hole, a public thank you in a staff briefing or, if they've really gone the extra mile (or even just completed the tasks they have been paid to do really well), then a nice box of chocolates or bunch of flowers. Saying thank you acknowledges that you have appreciated their efforts and that you don't take them for granted. I know that I am always much more ready to help out somebody in the future if they've taken the time to properly thank me for my previous contribution!

Section XI

Preparation for Inspection

Chapter 33

An Inspector Calls!

One thing to remember about preparation for inspection is that you can't just stay up really late the night before and tick off tasks that you were supposed to do over the last three years so that you are 'inspection ready'. The whole point of inspection is to highlight what the state of the school and the pupils' learning is – not just at a given time (that isolated snapshot of two days of actual inspection) but across time.

Inspectors seek to find out what teaching and learning, behaviour, standards, achievement and leadership are typically like over a period of time. Therefore, if you've been following the advice in this book up to this point you should be sorted! Of course, pupils give things away if teachers suddenly start teaching differently. Even if students don't give the game away willingly, their reaction or lack of familiarity with the teaching techniques or teacher systems will be obvious to the seasoned inspector. So what I'm trying to say is, you can't pull the wool ...

Now I am presuming that you have been following the advice given; however, these are the top ten things you can do. They are not an exhaustive list though – that's what the rest of this book is about:

1. **Look at all classrooms with fresh eyes**

    Are there shabby displays, broken blinds that obscure the whiteboard, things that should have been fixed?

Get them sorted. Ask your team if they have every-thing they need to teach good lessons. Pupils having to share resources too much, not having dictionar-ies in rooms so they can't look up the meanings of words, constant interruptions because staff members are borrowing items from each other – all of these undermine good teaching and learning and are simple to put right. Are there piles of old work and exercise books in the room? Don't have these hanging about. By all means keep examples of great work, but expect inspectors to gather evidence everywhere!

2. **Ensure that books and work are marked thoroughly**

Most inspectors usually look at books or work that the pupil is actually using in the class because this repre-sents a true picture of their learning. If you are asked to provide a sample of books for the inspection team look over them first before you hand them in! I have always been shocked when books with poor or miss-ing marking have been handed in by the SMT/head of department. If you have an unusual system, such as rough work books or work in folders, make sure that this is made clear to the inspection team so that they know they are seeing draft books (also show their redrafted work). Ideally, if you have been following the advice in Chapter 23, books should have a simple marking policy or guidelines stuck in the front so par-ents and inspectors who aren't subject specialists will understand the assessment process.

3. **Data – you need to know how your subject has been achieving across time**

Ofsted look at three years of data to determine trends. Have this to hand and be able to explain any dips or weaknesses in your data. Don't just rely on external tests or examinations – what do your most recent internal tests or assessments show? It is important to have accurate current data for your groups, particularly if your SMT is trying to persuade inspectors that last year's results were an aberration and that currently pupils are doing much better. Be prepared to talk about these at group level and be able to discuss individuals to show how they are progressing. If your department is appealing about any examination results, make sure you know how many pupils this is for and, if the appeal is upheld, how this will affect your data.

4. **What is working? What have you done? Why have you done it? What's the impact?**

    Be prepared to talk about what you have done to improve teaching and learning and standards across your team. You might find it helpful to do a SWOT analysis on a single sheet of A4 paper to help focus your mind.

5. **Have records on the training that your staff have undertaken and its impact**

    Staff might also be asked what CPD they have attended and whether it led to an improvement in their lessons/results – are they able to talk about what they did and what impact it had?

6. **Know your groups and pupils**

    Staff need to know their students really well. Many schools have found it useful to have a colour coded seating diagram showing where pupils sit and their individual abilities and any specific needs that they might have. Even if it is very early in the school year, inspectors will expect staff to know their pupils as individuals and plan for them accordingly.

7. Remind staff to plan effective lessons but to be confident enough to divert from the lesson plan if they need to

Inspectors will be judging the quality of teaching and learning in the lesson, rather than evaluating the neatness of the lesson plan. Ensure that staff expect inspectors to move around the room, talking to pupils and looking at work. They may also be asked questions about the lesson or any other 'inspection trail' the inspector is gathering evidence on; for example, they might be asked questions about behaviour, training opportunities or the support they receive from the SMT – whatever issues the inspector is following up.

8. Be prepared to observe lessons with the inspectors or talk about your team

So be prepared to be asked who should be observed to see some really good sixth form/GCSE/PE lessons. You should be aware of how staff typically teach, but also be prepared to give a judgement on an individual lesson with an inspector by your side. Remember here that you are looking at the learning in the lesson, evaluating how much pupils are progressing. Make sure you look at all the pupils, take the opportunity to ask them about what they are learning and look at their books. Inspectors might want to see how effectively you give feedback to your staff. Remember, it is about supporting your comments with evidence – if groups of pupils are off task the lesson won't be good. Your school will have a lesson observation pro forma, but it doesn't hurt to download a copy of the current inspection framework and evaluation schedule from Ofsted (www.ofsted.gov.uk). This is what inspectors use to guide their judgements and this means you will have the version which is most up to date.

9. **Make snacks and coffee available**

Staff are likely to be tense and burning up more energy when they are faced with the prospect of scrutiny. The constant pressure of feeling that you will be observed next is very daunting. Make sure that there is a good supply of healthy snacks in the office, such as bananas and cereal bars, to keep everybody going and raise spirits.

10. **Exude calm and confidence**

Tell your staff that you have every confidence in them! Acting like a headless chicken won't help matters and often the key to teaching good lessons is about feeling confident to adapt and change your lesson if it isn't working. Expect staff to give lesson plans to inspectors (although this is not mandatory the process of planning and thinking through the lesson is essential in helping them plan for good learning). Make sure staff also have pupils' assessment data to hand.

Section XII

Making Time Work for You!
Key Time Management Tips

Chapter 34

Time Management

We all have the same amount of time in a day; however, some middle leaders appear to manage their time much more effectively than others. They achieve more, always meet deadlines and, importantly, they also have some time for themselves.

Myth 1: Working harder is always the answer

An outstanding middle leader isn't necessarily the person who puts in the most hours – often these are far from the best. Working ever harder and spending longer and longer at school can surprisingly decrease our effectiveness rather than increase it. If we are too tired and stressed, if we get anxious over completing every last thing, we will find ourselves getting overtired, bad tempered and even ill or burnt out. Overworking doesn't lead to a harmonious time for your team members – or your family and friends out of school.

Why not try: really focusing on the task in hand. Set an egg timer or your mobile alarm and see how much of the task you can get done in thirty minutes. Focusing on a task without checking email/Facebook/Twitter can seriously increase your productivity and give you some important downtime too. Set yourself a cut off time so that you know you don't have all evening to complete the task – you have exactly an hour and a half! You'll be surprised by how much you can get done when you really focus.

Myth 2: There is an ideal time management system

When I ask middle leaders on training courses if they are effective at managing their time I get a range of answers. One Science coordinator looked quite distressed and said, 'I am hopeless at time management. I always leave things to the last minute. I really need a deadline to motivate me. I am a failure.' When I asked her if she always met deadlines, she said she did. She just had a different approach to the person next to her who liked to think about things and complete them well in advance, rather than needing the shot of adrenaline that working right up to the deadline brings.

There isn't one way of managing your time. What works for some staff might not work for you.

Why not try: different times and styles of working. Setting deadlines, staying late/getting in early/working at lunch. Mix it up and ask other staff for their strategies until you find a preferred system. Keep a careful diary of your time. What are your 'time thieves'? Is it Facebook/gassing with friends before going home/spending hours recreating resources because you have an inefficient filing system? Knowing what or who your time thieves are and your preferred style of working will help you become more productive. I found that twenty minutes of quiet working at the start of the day before the bell – while I was fresh and before I had tired myself out after a day teaching – was worth fifty minutes of working at the end of the day! However, this might not work for you. Do what is best for you – but do experiment.

Myth 3: Great middle leaders have to do things perfectly

We want to have high standards and we want to do things to a very good degree. However, you mustn't let 'the perfect be the enemy of the good'. By this I mean you might not think you can write the ideal or perfect scheme of work/lesson plan/Gifted and Talented intervention, so you think, 'I had better just leave it as it is and not bother doing it because I haven't got time to make it perfect.'

Aiming for perfection all the while isn't healthy. It isn't realistic in teaching. Trying to do things to the best of your ability is good, but sometimes you have to say, 'This is good enough. It isn't perfect, but it is probably pretty good. Let's see how it goes and we can always improve it later.' Striving for perfection isn't desirable; also, when you think you have spent hours getting things 'perfect', then you won't want to amend and improve them and often this is very necessary. Working for a middle leader who demands perfection from herself and others is also very stressful for staff. We can't be perfect all of the time and we shouldn't try to be.

Why not try: using and amending ideas from other schools or the Internet, rather than believing you have to create everything from scratch. Unless you are planning to sell your resources or write a book, then things do not have to be original. Adapting and personalising existing tools or schemes can be a very effective time saver. If someone has already done it to a high degree then personalise it and adapt it to suit your context.

Myth 4: Great leaders need to do it all themselves!

Sometimes it is very important to roll up your sleeves and get stuck in; to show that you are not afraid of hard work.

Delegation, however, is key in being a good leader, especially if you are leading a core subject. Think about delegating tasks at home too if you have willing family members or see if you can outsource some of them. When I was a middle leader I paid for a cleaner to spend two hours cleaning my house each Friday. I started the weekend knowing that I would not have to clean the bathroom, hoover or mop the floor. It didn't cost a great deal, but it meant that Friday night was a positive experience: the house was clean and fresh, ready for the weekend. This meant that when I did spend some of Sunday working or supermarket shopping I could still have some 'free time' and I used this to do the things I wanted to do rather than cleaning.

We've discussed the strategies for effective delegation in Chapter 32 and I would suggest you remind yourself of them. Remember: don't leave delegating until things have become an emergency.

Often leaders don't want to delegate tasks because they fear losing control or that other people won't complete the task to the same degree of competence. A good leader realises that developing people is a key part of their role. It takes time to skill somebody up, but this is time worth investing.

Saying no nicely

This sounds a bit negative, but it is pretty near the top of my own personal list of time-saving techniques. Nothing manages your time better than saying 'No'. As a new middle leader I started out as a real 'people pleaser', doing more and more, whether it was for people in my department or for the SMT or just for friends and acquaintances. Now, I am a big fan of helping people out, but there's a fine line between supporting your staff and doing their jobs for them.

A member of the SMT noted that I was working late one day and asked if at four thirty I would do her a favour as she had to get home early that night. She wanted me to supervise the 'clubs' bus. 'Of course,' I said. It took over twenty minutes, but I was happy to help. She asked me the next two weeks. This became a habit (using up over twenty minutes of my time when I wanted to be finishing off things or marking), until a wise member of staff told me that the member of the SMT was paid an additional allowance for completing this duty and now she hadn't done it for over a month! The next week, as she swanned by me in the corridor, she said, 'Alright if you do my extra-bus duty again?' She seemed quite surprised when I said it wasn't because I was busy. I had been spending twenty minutes doing somebody else's job for over a month. I could have spent that time working and gone home twenty minutes earlier – in future I did.

Reflection moment

Help people out, but don't create a dependency or allow yourself to be taken advantage of. A bit of give and take is important and you don't want to be a mean spirited person; however, when you are asked to do something you need to think: is this my job, will this help me move my department on and is it linked with my priorities? Or is it somebody trying to get me to do their job for them? If you find somebody frequently asks favours of you, feel free to ask for one in return. I could have said, 'Yes, I am happy to do that bus duty for you. How about we swap it and you do my Friday night detention!' People think twice about always asking for a favour if you often expect one back.

Tips for saying no nicely

It has taken me years and years to do this effectively, but it is a massive time saver. You need to maintain good relationships with people, but sometimes saying no nicely is key to your own well-being and key to ensuring that you are focusing on the right priorities for you and your department.

Offer them someone else

People often just want the job doing, they don't really care who does it. However, if you are known as a people pleaser/really organised/hard worker you might get more than your fair share of extra requests. Helping out is fine, but being somebody's 'go to guy' for every naff job is not. It is important to set some boundaries!

If you just say 'I am too busy at the moment,' they might keep on at you until you say yes. Say no firmly, but suggest somebody else. 'Running a parental forum sounds interesting, but I can't do this. Might this be up John's street or part of Ben's responsibility as Year 8 head?' Giving up somebody else's name is a key way of fending off unwanted extra jobs.

Ask what can be taken off you

If your line manager wants you to take on yet another initiative or task and you feel stuck, then list some of the tasks that you are already committed to: 'I'm overseeing the school newspaper and the debating club at the moment, as well as taking part in the boys' working party, and you've also asked me to mentor the new head of Drama so I am doing that too. Which one of these would you like me to drop/would you take off me, to allow me to complete your new project?' This is a good line as it highlights what you are already doing (thereby showing you are already pulling your weight) and will allow the other person to reassess their priorities. If their new task is absolutely urgent then they will tell you some other task you can drop or you might get more time/support, but more often than not the new 'urgent' task will pass to someone else or they will decide it isn't that urgent after all!

Sometimes you will want to take on new things

These can be a really good way of building your experience, developing new ideas and furthering your career. However, once something is added to your list be careful that it doesn't always remain there. Yes, you might like to get involved in running the whole school initial teacher training, but is this a permanent task or for one year only? Will you receive any extra time or funding? If you have been in charge of something for several years and you know you won't gain anything extra for doing it again, then be willing to give up other responsibilities rather than keep adding to them. This way you keep your sanity, and the task or responsibility that you are now bored of could well be the 'career opportunity' that somebody else is waiting for, so pass it on!

Chapter 35

Top Tips from Successful Middle Leaders

1. **Start the day doing the task that you have the most resistance to**

   Completing a task that you don't want to do really gets you motivated for the day ahead. This is not a popular tactic, but it is effective!

2. **Buy a notebook to plan tasks and record when you have done them**

   Make sure that you aren't always just responding to other people's 'urgent' requests – ensure you allow time for focusing on your own priorities. Recording them helps remind you that they are important and will help you chart progress.

3. **Spend some time planning your priorities at the beginning of the week**

   Taking fifteen minutes on a Sunday planning your week ahead can really make a difference. It means that you can ensure you are clear about your various tasks and priorities for the coming week. One head of department I know draws a mind map while watching her son at swimming practice on a Sunday. It has different strands for her teaching, leadership in department, her time, her family concerns, and whole school priorities. She then uses this in the week to check that she is spending her time fairly dealing with each area. This helps her ensure that the week doesn't just become about her own lessons or the department – it means she gets a balance between each area, including her own well-being and home life.

4. Schedule in time for yourself

This can include exercise time, time with your family or time for your own hobbies or other commitments. Put this in your diary in a specific colour. Having an empty looking diary is seen as carte blanche by some people for filling it up for you! If you can turn to the diary in a meeting and say, 'I'd love to help at the Year 6 disco, but it looks like I am already busy that Friday night.' Nobody needs to know that the code DLGT between 5 'til late is really code for 'drinking lots of gin and tonic'! I have frequently had my diary filled up for me by others through opening it at inopportune times in meetings – not any more. I now have my colours and secret codes!

5. Make good use of ICT to help support you

Dropbox is a great tool for storing and sharing resources. Emails can be checked and replied to by phone. Shopping and banking can be quickly sorted online – obviously not when you are teaching though! Choose what works for you to allow you to manage your time most effectively. There are some really useful apps and online resources. We often have odd ten- or fifteen-minute gaps where we are waiting for a meeting to start or travelling to school by train. How could we use this time more efficiently?

6. Manage your use of emails and requests

People who send lots of emails receive a lot of emails. Limit your use of them. Understand when you don't need to send a response to somebody. If somebody catches you in the staffroom and keeps asking you to email non-vital information to make their lives easier, ask them if they want to drop by your office so you can find it for them. The chances are they won't. People love creating work for other people, but they don't often like doing it themselves: use this as a tool to thin out requests.

When I first started running training courses, delegates would often ask me if I could just email them a specific resource, idea or link. Sometimes I would return home from a day's training with over twenty sticky notes full of requests from individuals. Some of their handwriting was appalling and it could take me an entire evening or longer to go through them, finding and sending the right resource – and occasionally it bounced back because the email wasn't right. Many people didn't even say thank you after I had done this.

I realised I was spending a vast amount of my downtime doing this. This was time I could have been working on other projects or kicking back and relaxing after a crazy day. Now I like to be helpful, and I realise that some people really wanted and appreciated my efforts, but some people seemed to be asking for things just for the sake of it! When training, I still get people asking me if I can send them links or resources but now I say, 'Of course, but you need to email me and request it.' I initially did this because it would save me finding the right email address – but what has actually happened is that although fifteen people might ask for something verbally, only three will actually bother to follow up and email me to ask for it. These are the

people who really want it and the effort of emailing
has been done by them; now this task of following up
takes me a few minutes instead of several hours and
the people who really want help still get it.

Thinking point

- Which tasks do you hate doing around the house?
  Which of these could you outsource? How much do
  you value your time? (If you could pay someone to do
  something that would gain you an extra few hours,
  how much would it be worth to you?)

- What takes up most of your time? Is this linked to
  your priorities?

- What are your 'time thieves'? Why not log the interruptions over a couple of days?

- Which resources or ideas have you adapted from
  other people?

- Perfection or good enough? Think about the tasks you
  are involved in. Which ones need to be done 'perfectly'
  and which ones can be 'good enough'?

- When did you last say no? Should it be more often?

- Can you fill the odd spare ten minutes with a useful task?

- Look at your job description and main role – are you
  doing any tasks that you have just 'inherited', tasks that
  you shouldn't really be doing?

- Are your personal and department systems and filing
  mechanisms effective so that you can quickly retrieve
  the correct information and resolve situations?

Middle Leader Challenges and Next Steps

Chapter 36

Dealing with Difficult People

66 A leader takes people where they want they want to go.
A great leader takes people where they don't necessarily
want to go, but ought to be.

Rosalynn Carter, US First Lady 1977–1981 99

Now I could write a book on this topic alone, and many useful ones have been written, including the *Anger and Conflict Management Pocketbook* by Paul Blum, amongst many others. If you are following all of the other advice in this book which relates to managing your team successfully, then the number of issues with difficult people should be greatly reduced.

However, you might have heard of the 'Pareto Principle' (based on the work of an Italian economist), which relates to the fact that, in life, 20% of something is always responsible for 80% of the results. It is often known as the 80–20 rule. So 20% of the clothes in your wardrobe get used in 80% of your outfits, 20% of pupils in school cause 80% of the discipline issues, and so on. It is also the case with people in your team. In a department of ten you will find it is probably only one or two (and the same people) that cause you persistent and repeated problems, sapping your energy and enthusiasm. So what can you do?

I am going to make some suggestions that have worked for me. Many situations are common across schools and in leading teams across the wider world of work. Of course, you will need to use your own skill and judgement to decide how to deal with things and when, if necessary, to refer things up to your SMT link – knowing when *you* should deal with things and when it is right to escalate issues is important. You don't want your SMT link thinking that they are doing all of your work, but neither do you want to hold on to issues where you should be referring them. Here are some strategies I have found useful as 'prevention is better than cure':

1. **Appointing staff**

   This is your chance to prevent future problems, ensuring that you've got a positive, hard-working and effective member of staff on your team rather than a moany, incompetent, draining one who will cause you problems. Always, always get them to teach a lesson during the interview and you should select the topic so that they don't just trot out a tested interview lesson that they've borrowed from another teacher or downloaded from the Internet!

   Make sure you get to ask some interview questions that really get them to think on their feet. This will show how they react under pressure and whether they can solve problems or if they will always come running straight to you to sort things out for them. Make sure, though, that you don't add too many of these challenging questions as they can be off-putting for the interviewee!

   Some head teachers can be so keen to fill the post that they might encourage you to accept a staff member when you can just tell they won't be good enough for the role. If the staff member isn't right (and you can't persuade the head not to appoint), ask whether they can be put on a temporary contract so you have a chance to see what they are like over time. Are your misgivings well founded or do they rise to the challenge and impress you?

Finally, when recruiting I always put a great store by the attitude of the candidate; if they are well qualified but start laying the law down in the interview about what they are or aren't willing to do, then alarm bells will ring. I might be more impressed by a less qualified candidate with a super keen attitude, and one who knows that they have a lot to learn and who will be willing to put in the effort and take advice on how to improve. Teachers with the right mindset can definitely improve their skills over time and learn about new areas of the curriculum – but their attitudes and work ethic are often set! Look for flexibility and the type of attitude staff have before you appoint. Preventing mistakes when making appointments is much easier than trying to undo them once you've appointed a problem person!

2. **Your communication and management style**

    Make sure that you don't cause problems for yourself by being a poor communicator or by letting a little power go to your head. Other people have skills and experience to offer. If they detect that you are not interested in their ideas and that you are a power-crazed megalomaniac then they will feel resentful.

3. **Listening and being available**

    It can be super frustrating when staff don't do things the way you want them to or team members deliberately choose to misinterpret your request (this is a subtle form of sabotage). Ensure that before you start off any new initiative or idea that you listen carefully to their views and that you are clear on why things need to happen. Make sure that you are frequently available to deal with teething problems and queries. It is when you are persistently unavailable that people revert to the old way of doing things, make changes because you weren't about or take refuge in moaning and spreading dissent.

4. Becoming non-stick coated!

Don't expect everyone to agree with you all of the time. This is a crucial piece of advice. There will be dissenters and people who like to disagree with whatever you have suggested. There may be all manner of reasons for this: they may be habitually grumpy, jealous of your role or just see that changes mean work for them.

Remember you are not aiming to win a popularity contest – your job is to lead the department effectively so that pupils get the best deal possible. This may ruffle some feathers – I'd be surprised if it didn't. Yes, it would be great if everybody in the team had you right at the top of their Christmas card list, but this is not your reason for being. You've got to do the right thing and that will mean managing some disagreements and not getting downhearted if everybody doesn't always leap in and say it's a great idea when you first suggest something!

Being 'non-stick coated' is important as it means that once you have decided something is a good idea (and you have the evidence for it) you can follow this through and not allow other people's negativity to put you off course. In one job I had to make some difficult changes and I knew that people wouldn't always like them; in fact, one team member advised me that the previous team leader had been so popular because 'she just left us to our own devices'. This wasn't going to happen and I knew that I would face some resentment for improving working practices. When I had some very difficult 'chats' and meetings, I had a particular jacket and I would wear it thinking: 'I am doing the right thing. I'm non-stick coated in this jacket – I'm a leader and the attitude of the negative 20% won't stick or wear me down.' Over time things improved, changes happened, people got used to new ways of working and I found I had to mentally repeat, 'I am non-stick coated,' much less often. A great leader does the right thing, even if it might make them temporarily unpopular with a vocal minority in their team.

5.   Being calmly persistent

Being persistent is an important skill in dealing with difficult people. Sometimes staff will try and throw a strop or will be deliberately difficult just to see if you will back off. Being known as a 'stroppy individual' in a team has some advantages if it means that your line manager will avoid asking you to do your fair share or will fail to have difficult conversations with you.

The secret to dealing with stroppy exploders, whether they are parents, pupils or tricky staff members, is not to explode in a similar way. When dealing with unpredictable or aggressive people it is very important to stay absolutely calm and to repeat the request in a clear way, even if they are blustering. The broken record repeating requests can take the wind out of the most difficult person. They are often sounding off, hoping to start an argument with you or hoping to dissuade you from following through.

Staying calm really stops them in their tracks. I was reminded of this recently when I saw a teacher dealing with a hostile and very angry Year 10 student in the corridor. The pupil was really sounding off about something; their voice was loud and their body language was aggressive. The teacher remained calm, softly spoken and repeated, 'I need you to give me your phone, Jason.' She refused to get engaged with the bluster and arguments that Jason was presenting, instead repeating like a broken record, 'I need you to give me your phone, Jason,' and eventually, with a sigh and a huff, he passed over his phone. Staying calm and measured is always the answer, whether it is a parent wanting to debate whether Claire should complete her detention or Mrs Fluffy complaining about the Year 8 reports deadline when she's got so much else to do – acknowledge that she is busy, but reiterate that the reports are still needed at this time. 'I know that you are busy, Mrs F – but the reports *are* needed by Wednesday.'

More problems

1. Don't make presumptions

Imagine this scenario: You don't receive a birthday card from your best friend. What is the most likely reason for this omission? Is it:

a. They've forgotten
b. They're angry with you
c. The card is lost in the post
d. They've lost their diary

Now the answer could, of course, be any of the four possible scenarios or even plenty more, but one of the problems is we tend to presume and imagine we know what other people are thinking. We often come up with answers that are very far from the truth and this can lead to us acting and treating this person in a particular way. This can cause us problems with our relationship. If we imagine that our friend's card is lost in the post we are likely to react very differently to if we imagine that she has fallen out with us over some possible slight.

The same is true when we are managing our teams. We must be careful not to attribute reasons to actions without evidence; instead we must speak to people about any issues, real or perceived. Don't presume that some team members won't want to get involved in things and others will, because it will reinforce your negative and positive views of individuals. If Gill looks cross at the start of the team meeting, should you take it as a personal slight, or could she be thinking about a tricky class, whether she's got food in for dinner tonight or a difficult issue with her teenage son? A good team leader ensures that they don't just presume and that they seek evidence for their views.

2. **Don't gossip**

Some teams brew gossip and backbiting. As a team leader you set the tone, and some individuals might try to curry favour with you by sharing or starting gossip. This is divisive and can cause factions within a team. Rise above it (however juicy the gossip might be!) and don't get involved!

3. **Don't have favourites**

Some team members will be more likeable and work harder than others. Your personality will chime more with some team members than others; however, you need to treat everybody fairly. Clearly NQTs and student teachers should get some special consideration because they are at the start of their careers and will need special guidance, but value everybody equally. Don't give the plums to your mates, be professional. Feeling that you aren't liked or treated fairly by your team leader is one of the biggest criticisms I hear about leaders. If you have ever been on the receiving end of not being one of the chosen few then it can be very isolating and lead to resentment and backbiting. We are programmed to like people who are similar to us in outlook and situation but make sure that you don't build a team of 'mini yous'. Everybody has something to offer – find it and try to involve them in the team. Even if they always decline your offers of attending the sixth form theatre trip, or the Year 7 workshop or reception visit, the fact that you have offered means they won't say that you are unfair and, who knows, they might surprise you.

4. Don't make things personal

There is a tendency to see some people as negative because they often are. However, try not to constantly criticise people because it's very demotivating and makes them become even more cynical and disheart- ened. If you do have an issue with someone, or a complaint about them, seek to redress it in a profes- sional manner. Talk to them about their behaviour or practice; don't criticise them as a person. For example, 'Ben Jones' mother said that you have not set any homework this term?' and awaiting their response is preferable to being vague or generally negative about their professionalism. Try to speak factually rather than emotionally, and allow the other person their say. It might be that there is a very good reason why home- work was not set or there may be some temporary reason why they have let their standards slip. This still needs addressing, but it is important to listen to them first.

5.   Provide support

Sometimes people are difficult or confrontational because they are finding teaching tough or they are not coping in their personal life. Teaching can be a very stressful job and some teachers might not want to admit that they are drowning in the workload, feeling under pressure or at their wits' end about how to ensure their Year 6 meet their targets. This can lead to them lashing out or becoming withdrawn because of these issues and therefore difficult to manage.

Developing a good relationship with your team members as individuals means that you can detect when they are feeling less resilient and they are more likely to speak out before it becomes an insurmountable issue. You might be able to suggest some strategies to help them manage their workload (see pages 231–234 for examples), arrange some training or coaching – particularly if they are in the first few years of their career – or provide a listening ear.

Ask for advice from the SMT

Of course, you are not the font of all wisdom, but recognising the signs when somebody is stressed and under pressure, talking to them and maybe asking advice from your SMT link is useful. The Teacher Support line[1] also offers some useful online and free telephone resources that can help provide sound, unbiased advice for you or your staff. As a line manager we have a duty of care to our team to look out for their well-being, both mentally and physically.

---

[1] See www.teachersupport.info

Unfortunately, there are staff who might be under-achieving not because they feel overwhelmed but because they can't be bothered. Recognising why somebody might be underachieving is important and you need to discuss with your SMT the appropriate action to take. If Ben hasn't completed his reports because he is completely stressed out, feeling very ill, and spent all weekend trying to write the perfect lesson plan, then he will need a different approach to Jane, who has not completed them because she can't be bothered and it is her third set of late reports. Knowing when to give a helping hand and offer support so that staff can improve and when to call someone to account is important.

6. People are motivated by different things

Remember, people in your team will be motivated by different things. Tapping into this can be useful in avoiding conflict. Some staff members really like to feel that they are helping you and will respond well to requests that show that they are personally valued by you. Some need public kudos and acclaim for what they do; others are motivated purely by the positive responses the pupils give them; others are set on forging ahead and building a career. Knowing what motivates your staff can help you get the best out of them (this also works in avoiding conflict).

Some people get very stressed by change; others get stressed by not knowing the nitty-gritty detail and specifics about things; others get very stressed about looking too far into the future. Knowing what presses the buttons of your team members as individuals and who works well together is crucial in helping you to manage your team and avoid unnecessary stress and strain. One of the biggest mistakes a team leader can make is to presume that everybody will think the same way as they do. Remember, your team is made up of various different individuals who will have varying degrees of expertise and different flaws and strengths. As a team leader you need to use your ability to make this varied group gel together and work effectively as both individuals and as a team.

Everybody who manages a team will face challenges and problems – if they didn't, then there wouldn't be the need for a team leader. It is important not to be daunted and downhearted by these challenges but to think carefully about how you can try and avoid them in the first place or resolve them. Sometimes the people who are in your team aren't the ones who are actually causing you the issues – it might be your SMT link, an external consultant that your academy has foisted on you or a pesky governor who wants to know what you are doing. The next chapter deals with the issues inherent in 'managing up'.

Chapter 37

Managing Up! Dealing with Your Senior Leadership Link, Governors and Consultants

Dealing with your department members is one thing; you are their line manager and have some experience or expertise in this area. You should therefore feel that you have some confidence in dealing with the issues related to these relationships. However, dealing with your deputy head (who is your line manager), the link governor or external consultants can be a much more daunting matter.

Managing up!

Members of the SMT come in all sorts of packages: most are experienced and supportive, but many are not specialists in your subject area. You therefore need to learn how to 'manage up' so that you have a good relationship with them and understand how to 'manage' them effectively.

A good SMT line manager will meet frequently with you and will be a helpful guide. You need to develop a good degree of trust between you because you need to be able to use them as a sounding board for your ideas and plans for your team. You need to be able to discuss your concerns honestly so it is important to build a constructive relationship.

If your actions and behaviour are clearly motivated by the fact that you have the very best interests of your pupils at the heart of what you are doing then this will help.

A good SMT link

You will know if you have a proactive line manager because they will arrange to meet with you regularly, listen and pose questions, talk through things you should be doing, point out improvements you could be making, provide suggestions and solutions for dealing with difficulties and occasionally challenge you.

If your SMT link is not as proactive as they might be you may need to take the lead and 'manage' them. They can be very busy and while you may take it as a compliment if they leave you to get on with it, they do have a role in helping you do the best job possible. So if they are busy, besieged or are overly laid back about arranging things, you will need to take the initiative.

Do:

- Talk through your action plans with them and ask for specific advice.

- Ask them to come and do some joint lesson observations or learning walks with you to moderate your judgements of your team's lessons.

- Talk to them about your monitoring process and the impact it is having.

- Ask for advice about dealing with tricky problems and underachieving staff.

- Keep some notes of the meetings so you know what you have discussed and follow up actions that you have both agreed to do.

- Identify solutions – busy senior leaders like solutions not problems! They don't want to be doing your job for you, but it is a good idea to keep them informed. Explain the problem clearly, say why it is a concern and provide a clear solution. For example, say, 'Staff in my team admit that they lack confidence in teaching higher ability pupils,' and offer a suggested strategy. 'I would like to arrange an afternoon's training for them. Most of us are free on Thursday afternoon. It would cost £600 pounds, and I could evaluate the impact by doing a follow-up lesson observation and survey.'

- Explain your reasoning behind your key decisions.

- Ask for further funding or resources. Be specific; investigate what you want and explain how it will help. The SMT often have lots of different pots of money that you might be unaware of, particularly in state schools. These are often for specific interventions, raising achievement, CPD, etc. If you know something needs doing and it will cost, ask if there is any funding available.

- Champion the department's cause! If you feel Geography is getting a raw deal compared to other subjects explain why and have statistics to back up your ideas. One head of Geography I know was under pressure to improve results. They did need improving; however, pupils were persistently being taken out of Geography GCSE lessons to attend extra English or Maths classes. He charted this and showed exactly how many lessons were being lost – this resulted in a change in the way the school ran catch-up sessions.

- Ask them, 'Who else in the school is doing this better?' This will help highlight other areas of the school that are being successful in the area that you are trying to develop. Learning from others helps you avoid recreating the wheel. The SMT should know where the areas of good practice are.

- Ask them to give you specific advice – if they can't, make sure you have researched where you could go to receive the training, consultancy or the answer. If you need subject or exam-board specific guidance or consultancy have the name of the organisation ready and the price and get them to agree to it.

- Highlight the good things that are going on in your area and invite them to attend any extra- curricular events.

Don't:

- Be generally negative and complain about the school/department/others in the SMT – it will get back! Be precise if there are issues and offer your preferred solutions or ask advice.

- Expect them to have all of the solutions. You are an expert in your area. You know what needs to happen. Inform them how they can help or explain what you need to happen next.

- Agree with everything they say! The SMT often go on a lot of training and may come back with a bonkers idea that they've heard in the lunch queue, they think it is the latest thing! Like you should change exam board midway through the year because they've heard another board is easier. Or that your department should run revision sessions every day in half term. If they have an inappropriate idea, explain to them professionally why it won't work, but you need to have other options or solutions available. A good head of a team isn't a 'yes' person – but pick your battles.

- Give up! If there is a big issue, for example truancy or a department member persistently not marking books, then you need to keep raising it until something is done about it.

- Complain about your SMT link to your team – it is unprofessional. Most are good at their job, but I've certainly met about 10% that aren't. They might be lazy, smartly dressed power trippers, or they may be well meaning but ineffectual. Unfortunately, it is not unheard of for a poor middle leader in charge of a key department to be promoted out of the way to the SMT! Persist with them. Ironically, the lazier they are the more you can use this to your advantage as you can propose solutions and they will often agree because it is easier. Using the phrase 'Ofsted will expect …' often has a galvanising effect on the SMT, who won't want to be found lacking – but don't overdo this. If they still don't support you on a key issue though, like staff underperformance, then you need to be prepared to talk about this to another member of the SMT if the current avenue has been exhausted.

- Cover things up. If you haven't done something or you don't understand a request, ask. Covering up only creates bigger problems for you further along the line. If you've tried something and it has failed, talk this through with them. Maybe it was a bad idea or maybe it was a good idea and it was just not executed as well as it could have been.

Remember: your SMT link or line manager's role is to provide support to help you do the best job you can – make them earn their money!

Governors

When I was a subject leader I didn't always view the fact that we had a link governor in a positive light. They created more mini jobs to be added to my already long list of things to do: governors wanting to observe lessons, preparing a report for governors about my subject area, remembering to invite them to any celebrations or extra-curricular activities – all of these felt like extra tasks that I could well do without. I didn't make full use of my governor and did not regard them as a force for good – I was wrong!

I have friends (who have no experience in education) who are school governors and I have realised that I seriously missed opportunities in the way I dealt with my link governors. Governors might have little educational expertise but they have chosen to become a governor because they are interested in education and because they have a desire to give something back. They don't become governors to try and catch you out! Their intentions are good and they have some spare time, so make the most of them.

Think about how you might work with the governors to show your department's strengths and also to highlight any issues that might need addressing. This is particularly fruitful if you have one that is attached to your area or specialism. One of my friends had the ear of her link governor so the governor would often say, 'What about the languages department?' when the head teacher was discussing new buildings, resources or training. Her governor was certainly the MFL department's champion and felt very involved in the department.

My friend had showed off aspects of her department that were doing really well (pointing out improvements she had made), inviting them to events and arranging lesson observations. Her governor was impressed and amazed at how MFL teaching had changed over the years, but the subject leader didn't shirk the issues. She also pointed out the weaknesses, particularly where she felt the governor could help her cause: 'We could really do with more money for these resources,' or, 'Notice how we have to walk across the school every lesson because our classrooms are all over the school.' Her governor could also see that these were issues and was more than happy to raise them with the SMT, adding force to the middle leader's concerns and moving the subject further up the head teacher's priority list!

Remember that many governors have a huge range of skills from the world of work that can be utilised by the savvy middle leader. They might be willing to come in to judge competitions, be interviewed about their experiences by pupils or even just act as an extra pair of helping hands on a school trip. Of course, the more you involve them in the positive aspects of your department, the more they will feel included and motivated about your department and your leadership.

You are likely to be called on to write reports or give presentations to your governors about the achievements of your department. Yes, they will be interested in the headline figures and exam results, and this is increasingly the case as Ofsted makes governors more accountable; however, governors aren't usually educational specialists so avoid educational jargon when you discuss examinations and courses. You will find that by clearly explaining your plans, what you've done and its impact, and by promoting your department and getting them involved, you can make your governor a useful ally, as well as a critical friend.

Thinking point:

- Do I have a link governor attached to my area/ department?

- How could I get them further involved?

- Do they have any specific skills from their job or experi- ence that might be useful?

- What are the areas of the school I'd like to show off to them?

- How might they help the team as a 'critical friend'?

External consultants

 ... either you will reach a point higher up today, or you will be training your powers so that you will be able to climb higher tomorrow.

Friedrich Nietzsche

I've worked as a consultant in hundreds of schools and I have also had consultants working alongside me when I was a subject leader and Local Authority leader. There are several factors to bear in mind when you have a consult- ant working with you and your team. Firstly, are they a consultant that you know and have invited in, perhaps to support a struggling NQT with their behaviour manage- ment, or are they being foisted on you? If you have a good relationship with a knowledgeable consultant they can be incredibly useful. They can:

- Give a second opinion and be a critical friend casting an eye over what you have done, giving you feedback on what is working and what could be better.

- They can save you loads of time! Perhaps your deputy head is allowing you some time with a consultant to conduct some work scrutinies, schemes of work or to provide a clear way forward for a particular issue.

- Perhaps they are providing some very focused training for your department on an area of the curriculum you are developing or an area of teaching that your department is weak at. Maybe lesson observations have indicated that questioning is an issue for many staff and you are holding an evening training session where the consultant will train staff in strategies for improving their questioning skills.

- Perhaps they are running a subject-specific revision workshop for pupils or running some extra-curricular provision for G&T students.

- Maybe your SMT is asking them to provide an external validation or review of your team.

Obviously, if they are coming in to take the load off and run some revision sessions they will be welcomed with open arms. Here they are doing some jobs for you that will be helpful, add value and free you up to do other things. Your attitude might be different if they are coming in to externally evaluate your team! Some things to bear in mind are as follows:

- Ensure that the purpose of the visit is crystal clear. If you are inviting the consultant in, be really specific – if you are running training explain *precisely* what you want your team to get out of the training and how long they have to run it. Ideally speak over the phone to agree this and get them to agree to it in writing. This will prevent any misunderstanding. You want your team bursting with ideas and enthusiasm at the end of a twilight training session, skilled up and ready to teach

in new ways – not feeling like it was a waste of time
and money.

- Check that you have got the right person for the task.
  If you really need some specific A level training but
  the consultant's background is Key Stage 2/3 they are
  unlikely to be right for it. You might want to contact the
  exam board to send somebody specific. A good consultant will be able to provide references and examples of
  similar work they have done elsewhere.

- If they are coming in to help provide external evaluation, then how 'soft' or 'hard' will this be? For example,
  a consultant might conduct some paired lesson observations with a new middle leader where they discuss
  their judgements and verbal feedback is given to staff
  and the middle leader. This is a very different training
  approach to a consultant who is told to come in and
  prepare the team for an inspection and who will be
  writing a formal report for the school – make sure you
  know where you stand and what to expect!

- What exactly is included in the day? Will there be any
  follow up, will you be able to ask them for any extras
  or will you have to get everything completed within
  the day? If you only have a day, make the most of it!
  Make sure if staff are being observed that there is time
  available within the day for feedback – even if this is
  at lunchtime. Consultants will expect very full days so
  squeeze every minute out of them!

- If training is being undertaken will the consultant bring
  the photocopied materials or will you be expected to
  do it? If this is the case, always ask for it at least a week
  beforehand! Find out what equipment they will need
  and advise them to download any video clips they
  need from the Internet so they are not dependent on the
  school's Internet access.

- Be really clear about how to get to the school and where you are based – this is really important if you are a split site school. If the consultant is arriving late in the day, will there be parking? Make sure you offer some tea or coffee and if you are a school with a minuscule lunch break advise the consultant to bring their own lunch.

- Does the consultant have a current Criminal Records Bureau (CRB) check?

- Make sure you evaluate the work of the consultant and its impact. If you are running training, they should offer an external evaluation form for each member of staff. If your deputy tells you that one is coming in, always think about what the impact of this visit will be and plan accordingly.

If you find a good consultant they can be worth their weight in gold because they can use their experience and expertise to save you time and energy and put you on the right track. However, if you find that your school or academy is using a consultant who is not helpful, experienced or credible, speak up so the school can amend the situation. A good consultant should save you time and make your life much better – if they don't, then it is just an expensive way of spending time.

Thinking point

- Do I have any gaps in my knowledge or my team where a consultant/AST might be a useful way of improving things?

- Can I use my networks to identify a good consultant who might support me in leading improvements in my team?

Final Words

So what's stopping you becoming an amazing middle leader? You've read the book and taken on board plenty of advice and useful tips. But remember: although leaders share many similar traits, no two leaders are exactly the same. It is up to you to trial things, to experiment and take on board some of the advice that you have found useful and to make it your own.

We've all been led by people and we remember those that did it well and also how they made us feel. As Lao Tzu, the Chinese philosopher, said: 'A leader is best when people barely know he exists, when his work is done, his aim fulfilled, they will say: we did it ourselves.'

You are on your journey to becoming an amazing middle leader – enjoy the ride and let me know how it turns out for you!

Further Reading and Resources

Top 5 books and resources for middle leaders:

1. *Head of Department's Pocketbook* by Brin Best and Will Thomas (Teachers' Pocketbooks, 2011). Useful, brief and nifty.

2. *Brilliant Teams: What to Know, Do and Say to Make a Brilliant Team* by Douglas Miller (Pearson Business, 2011). Business centred, but all the advice on running a team is applicable. There are also some useful sections on action planning.

3. *How Successful People Think* by John C. Maxwell (Center Street, 2009). An American business-based book but very useful and positive. It helps you to be creative in your thinking. It is very quick to read.

4. *Inspirational – and Cautionary – Tales for Would-be School Leaders* by Gerald Haigh (Routledge, 2007). Short stories from real life that exhibit management and leadership skills. It is insightful and thought-provoking rather than practical, but refreshing and interesting.

5. *Lesson Observation Pocketbook* by Roy Watson-Davies (Teachers' Pocketbooks, 2009). Ideas for getting the best out of lesson observations.

Top 5 books for improving teaching and learning:

1. *How to be an Amazing Teacher* by Caroline Bentley-Davies (Crown House Publishing, 2010). Classroom tips and strategies for the everyday classroom.

2. *The Perfect Ofsted Lesson* by Jackie Beere (Independent Thinking Press, 2012). Brief, concise and helpful.

3. *Whole School Progress the Lazy Way: Follow Me, I'm Right Behind You* by Jim Smith (Independent Thinking Press, 2012). For helping pupils become more independent.

4. *Evidence-Based Teaching: A Practical Approach (Second Edition)* by Geoff Petty (Nelson Thornes, 2009). Detailed and comprehensive.

5. *Outstanding Lessons Pocketbook* by Caroline Bentley-Davies (Teacher's Pocketbook, 2012). Some handy tips and teaching techniques for becoming outstanding.

Top 5 leadership books to help you become a senior manager:

1. *Leading in a Culture of Change* by Michael Fullan (Jossey Bass, 2007). An indispensable guide, written in a clear, readable style.

2. *The Perfect Ofsted Inspection* by Jackie Beere (Independent Thinking Press, 2012). Information about how to thrive, linked to the Ofsted framework.

3. *Literacy Across the Curriculum Pocketbook* by Caroline Bentley-Davies (Teachers' Pocketbooks, 2012). Tried and tested techniques to improve LAC in all subjects and to embed it across the whole school.

4. *Leadership with a Moral Purpose: Turning Your School Inside Out* by Will Ryan (Crown House Publishing, 2008). A useful and inspiring guide written by an ex-primary head teacher, but many of the premises and strategies are transferrable to leading any team.

5. *Managing Workload Pocketbook* by Will Thomas (Teachers' Pocketbooks, 2005). Some useful tips and practical techniques for managing a busy workload.

Top 5 websites for subject leaders

1. **Ofsted's own website: www.ofsted.gov.uk** Search for examples of good practice and to check out the latest requirements via the School Inspection Handbook.

2. **Department of Education: www.education.gov.uk** Information about statutory curriculum requirements and latest educational developments.

3. **Pearson: www.pearson.com** One of the largest publishers of curriculum resources and online support for pupils.

4. **Ofqual: www.ofqual.gov.uk** Information about examination requirements, reviews and changes.

5. **Times Educational Supplement website: www.TES.co.uk** Jobs, curriculum resources, forums and general education information.

Subject Associations

Each subject has a teachers' association that runs conferences, sells resources and usually has a useful website and a helpful magazine that subscribers receive. See if your department is signed up to one and ask if you can see their publications. Some of the main subject associations are listed below – but there will be others.

Art and Design

National Society for Education in Art and Design
www.nsead.org

Citizenship

Association for Teaching Citizenship
www.Teachingcitizenship.org.uk

Dance

National Dance Teachers Association
www.ndta.org.uk

Design and Technology

Design and Technology Association
www.data.org.uk

Economics and Business Studies

Economics, Business and Enterprise Association
www.ebea.org.uk

Geography

Geographical Association
www.geography.org.uk

History

The Historical Association
www.history.org.uk

English

National Association for the Teaching of English
www.nate.org.uk

IT

The national association for all those interested in technology in education
www.naace.org

Languages

Association for Language Learning
www.all-languages.org.uk

Physical Education

Association for Physical Education
www.afpe.org.uk

Music

The UK Association for Music Education
www.musicmark.org.uk

Mathematics

Association of Teachers of Mathematics
www.atm.org.uk

PSHE

PSHE Association
www.pshe-association.org.uk

Religious Education

The National Association of Teachers of Religious Education
www.natre.org.uk

Science

The Association for Science Education
www.ase.org.uk

Institute of Physics
www.iop.org

Index

About Caroline Bentley-Davies

Caroline Bentley-Davies is a freelance educational consultant and trainer. She has been a middle leader in three schools, a Local Authority adviser and an Ofsted inspector. She has run educational projects for the government and across networks of schools in the UK and overseas. She is the author of several books for teachers, including the bestsellers: *How to be an Amazing Teacher*, *Literacy Across the Curriculum Pocketbook* and *Outstanding Lessons Pocketbook*.

For more information about other books, training, speaking engagements or revision sessions for pupils that can be held at your school or college, please contact her directly:

caroline@bentley-davies.co.uk

or visit

www.bentley-davies.co.uk

Caroline runs a wide variety of training courses for teachers through various educational companies. Please see her website for details:

www.bentley-davies.co.uk

Ingram Content Group UK Ltd.
Milton Keynes UK
UKHW020227010423
419458UK00006B/47

9 781845 907983